JEWISH HEROES JEWISH VALUES

BARRY L. SCHWARTZ

* LIVING MITZVOT IN TODAY'S WORLD *

"The aim [of Jewish education] is to develop a sincere faith in the holiness of life and a sense of responsibility. . . ."
— MORDECAI KAPLAN

ACKNOWLEDGMENTS

I would like to extend special thanks to a number of individuals who helped with this project:

Adam Siegel, my editor at Behrman House, who enthusiastically received my proposal for this book, and whose many helpful suggestions helped shape both text and presentation.
Daniel Bial, for his professional expertise.
Debbie Bodin, who helped with some of my research.
My wife, Debby, for her encouragement.

This book is dedicated to my parents, Barbara and Rudy Schwartz, who first taught me about integrity and compassion, not to mention love.

The author and publisher gratefully acknowledge the cooperation of the following sources of photographs for this book:

Bill Aron: 1, 6 (left and right), 15, 19, 20 (left), 76, 77 (left), 100; Beth Hatefusoth, The Nahum Goldman Museum: 2 (right); The New York Public Library, Picture Collection: 2 (left); Bibliotheque Nationale: 5; Francene Keery: 6 (center); Academy/Devorah Preiss: 8 (right); Elaine Kadison Brown and Congregation B'nai Jeshurun: 8 (left); UPI/Corbis-Bettman: cover (center, upper right), 11, 12, 14, 28, 36 (right), 48, 51, 71, 83, 86, 88, 89, 92 (left), 101, 108, 109; Reuter/Corbis-Bettman: cover (bottom left), 17, 35, 44, 46, 60, 62, 63, 68, 94, 106, 113; YIVO: 20 (right), 44; Israeli Consulate: cover, 22, 102; Suzanne Kaufman/JTS: 25; NASA: 27; Jewish Theological Seminary: 30, 103; Tom McHugh/Photo Researchers, Inc.: 31; Robert F. Wagner, Labor Archives: 40; UJA Press Service: 43; Copyright by ANNE FRANK—Fonds Basel Switzerland: 52 (right); New York Public Library, General Research Division, Astor, Lenox and Tilden Foundation: 55; Philip Gendreau: 59; Brandeis University: 65; The Jerusalem Post: 69; World Wide Photos: 73, 110; Jewish National University Library: 74; Fred Stein: cover (upper left), 79, 111; Religious Action Center: 80; David James: 91, 92 (bottom right); Creative Image: 95; Yad Vashem: 97.

Book and Cover Design: PRONTO DESIGN & PRODUCTION, INC.

Library of Congress Cataloging-in-Publication Data

Schwartz, Barry L.
   Jewish heroes, Jewish values : living mitzvot in today's world /
Barry L. Schwartz.
     p.   cm.
   Includes bibliographical references and index.
   Summary: Presents biographies of famous Jewish men and women who have shown a commitment to upholding Jewish values. Includes activities for performing mitzvot.
   ISBN: 0-87441-615-9
   1. Jews—Biography—Juvenile literature. 2. Exempla, Jewish—Juvenile literature. 3. Ethics, Jewish—Juvenile literature. 4. Commandments (Judaism)—Juvenile literature. [1. Jews—Biography. 2. Commandments (Judaism) 3. Ethics, Jewish. 4. Conduct of life.]   I. Title.
DS115.S38   1996
920' .0092924—dc21
                        96-45441
                             CIP
                             AC

Published by
BEHRMAN HOUSE, INC.
235 Watchung Avenue, West Orange, New Jersey 07052

MANUFACTURED IN THE UNITED STATES OF AMERICA

Contents

Golda Meir

TZIONUT: *Zionism*

Sandy Koufax

K'LAL YISRAEL: *Jewish solidarity*

Hannah Senesh

OMETZ LEV: *Courage*

Introduction

MITZVAH. Quite possibly the most important word in Judaism.

Question: But what is a mitzvah?

　a. a good deed

　b. a commandment from God

　c. a Jewish responsibility

Answer: All of the above.

In order to lead meaningful lives and to make the world a better place, we must all assume many responsibilities, like visiting the sick, feeding the hungry, caring for the environment, taking care of the elderly, freeing those who are enslaved. Each of these is a mitzvah, a commandment from God. By performing mitzvot, we learn the proper way to live—how to treat others, our family, our friends, our community, our planet, and ourselves.

Question: What do mitzvot have to do with me?

Answer: You are what you do. Mitzvot are Jewish values in action. They teach us the Jewish way to live our lives—everything from observing Shabbat and celebrating the holidays to helping the homeless and supporting Israel. You will soon celebrate (or have recently celebrated) becoming a Bar or Bat Mitzvah. Judaism teaches that at that time you are old enough to begin taking on adult responsibilities. That means you are now ready to perform mitzvot.

Question: Where do the mitzvot come from?

Answer: We learn about mitzvot by studying the Torah. By Torah, I mean not only

Albert Einstein

TZEDAKAH: *Charity*

Henrietta Szold

PIKUAḤ NEFESH: *Saving a life*

Steven Spielberg

ZIKARON:*Remembrance*

the first five books of the Bible (Genesis, Exodus, Leviticus, Numbers, and Deuteronomy) but all the Jewish wisdom that has been handed down through the ages. This includes wisdom from the Bible, the Talmud, Midrash, even books and stories written in our own day.

After studying Torah, and learning about the mitzvot, we can put into action the Jewish values we have learned about. We may consider ourselves lucky to be able to do this for there was one time in our history when we almost lost the precious gift of Torah. About two thousand years ago, one man risked his life so that generations of Jews after him would be able to study Torah. His heroic act enabled us to continue the tradition of performing mitzvot.

Remembering the story of this brave man (whom you will read about in the first chapter), inspired me to think about other Jews (some of whom are still alive) who performed a courageous or heroic act that embodied a specific mitzvah.

Question: How will this book teach me about mitzvot?

Answer: This is a book about mitzvot and some great mitzvah doers. Heroes start out as ordinary women and men. What makes them special is their determination to accept responsibility and live according to high ideals. This path toward Jewish responsibility begins with mitzvot. I hope that these true stories will inspire you to become more responsible and to perform more and more mitzvot.

While I hope that the people portrayed in this book will serve as role models, this book is really designed to help you think about the mitzvot in your own life. Think about people you know who have fulfilled the different mitzvot in this book. Think about how you might have responded had you been in the hero's place. Finally, consider doing the activities (called Living the Mitzvah) that appear in each chapter. Doing these activities will help you take your first simple mitzvah steps.

It was once said that the only reason why we may see farther than our ancestors did is because we are standing on their shoulders. On the following pages are some inspiring shoulders to stand on. I hope that they will help you see farther, so that you may join in the Jewish people's efforts to repair and improve the world according to God's plan.

— Barry L. Schwartz

B·l·u·e·p·r·i·n·t

What to Look For in Each Chapter

SETTING THE SCENE
The time, place, and most important individuals in the story.

THE STORY
The hero and the event in his or her life that illustrates the mitzvah of the chapter.

EYEWITNESS TO HISTORY
A first-person account of the story, often written by the hero.

EXPLORING THE MITZVAH
The importance of the Jewish value and its connection to your life.

IN OUR ANCESTORS' FOOTSTEPS
A brief portrait of another hero in Jewish history who fulfilled the same mitzvah.

b · r · i · n · t

SPOTLIGHT ON THE BIBLE

A look at our biblical ancestors who embodied the mitzvah.

YOU ARE THERE

A journey back in time where you become a historic character from the story, or find yourself in a similar, contemporary dilemma.

LIVING THE MITZVAH

Activities to help you take your first simple mitzvah steps.

JEWISH HEROES HALL OF FAME

A review of what you have learned about the hero and an opportunity to explain how you can fulfill the mitzvah in your own life.

At the end of this book is a section entitled Keep Reading—a selection of books written about the people and events in each chapter. What better way to follow-up what you have learned in this book than by reading the biographies of these heroes and other inspiring stories? As you will find out in the first chapter, Jewish learning is a great mitzvah!

1

TALMUD TORAH תַּלְמוּד תּוֹרָה

THE MITZVAH OF JEWISH LEARNING

"Without Torah, a person stumbles. . . . With Torah, one walks like a person in the dark with a lantern."
—EXODUS RABBAH 36:3

Talmud Torah is the mitzvah of studying Torah. In this expression, the Hebrew word *Talmud* means "study." By studying the wisdom of our heritage, we learn how to direct our lives. Talmud Torah includes studying not only the Torah but all Jewish teachings.

GIVE ME YAVNEH AND ITS SAGES

Time: Nearly 2,000 years ago, in the year 69 C.E.

Place: Jerusalem

People: *Rabbi Yoḥanan ben Zakkai*: a famous rabbi;

Abba Sikra: a leading zealot and the rabbi's nephew;

Vespasian: the commanding general of the Roman army;

The Sages: leading rabbis who formed a center for Torah study and teaching

In the year 66 C.E., the vast Roman Empire stretched over 2,500 miles and comprised nearly all of the Western civilized world. For the previous 100 years, Rome's armies had spread out, conquering virtually the entire Mediterranean area, including most of southern Europe, northern Africa, and large parts of Asia Minor. Many countries had surrendered without

Vespasian, general of the Roman army.

With the rise of the Roman Empire, the Jewish people faced a serious threat to the survival of their religion. This detail from a replica of the Arch of Titus shows Romans in 70 C.E. triumphantly parading spoils from the Holy Temple in Jerusalem, which they had just destroyed.

a fight, recognizing Rome's superior forces. Others fought back and suffered extreme consequences. For example, after the Roman army conquered Carthage, an ancient city in North Africa, it killed all its citizens, leveled the city, and sowed salt in the ground so nothing would grow there.

Why did the Jews object so strongly to Roman rule?

Yet the Romans had never fully conquered Israel. For many decades, they had occupied Israel, but when they tried to force the Jews to obey Roman laws and follow the Roman religion, the Jews rebelled. The emperor Nero, fearful that revolution might spread outside Israel, sent one of his best generals, Vespasian, to quash the uprising.

The Jews fought back fiercely for four years, but the Roman army had more soldiers, better arms, and superior military knowledge. The Romans laid waste to much of the countryside, and in the year 69 C.E. the Romans demanded that the Jews surrender unconditionally or suffer the consequences.

How Jews Faced the Crisis

The Jewish people reacted to the Romans' threat in three ways. The first group of Jews, called collaborators, believed that they should comply with the Romans. They feared the Romans would kill all the Jews unless they surrendered. A second group of Jews, called zealots, believed that they should resist the Roman demands at all costs. These Jews felt that nothing was more important than remaining free Jews, even if doing so meant death.

A third group of Jews were known as compromisers. They argued that it was important to remain Jewish but that the only chance for the survival of the people was to work out some arrangement with Rome.

A Rabbi Takes Action

What were the advantages and disadvantages of collaborating with Rome?

According to the Talmud, Yohanan ben Zakkai was a rabbi esteemed for his wisdom. When the Romans laid siege to Jerusalem and threatened to destroy the city, he came up with a plan. Yohanan went to his nephew Abba Sikra, a zealot leader, and asked for his assistance in sneaking out of the city. Both knew the plan was extremely dangerous. The zealots had pledged to kill anyone who tried to deal with the enemy. Even if Yohanan escaped the wrath of the zealots, the Romans too might kill him.

The zealots were not letting anyone leave Jerusalem. But corpses had to be buried outside the city walls, so Yohanan pretended to be dead, and his students carried him outside the city. After his students reentered the city gates, the rabbi arose. He was soon arrested by Roman sentinels, and he asked to be taken to Vespasian.

When brought before Vespasian, Rabbi Yohanan predicted that the general was about to become emperor of Rome. Vespasian at first scorned the prediction, but when it came true, he granted the rabbi any one request. Rabbi Yoḥanan ben Zakkai is said to have replied, "Give me Yavneh and its sages." Yavneh was a small town near where Tel Aviv is today; it had a small academy dedicated to the study of the Torah.

Vespasian departed for Rome, leaving his son Titus in charge of the war against Israel. Within a year, Titus defeated Jerusalem's defenders. He destroyed the Temple, taking many of its holy objects, including the great menorah, back to Rome.

The small academy of Yavneh became the spiritual center of the Jewish people. For hundreds of years, Israel was under Roman control, but because of Yoḥanan ben Zakkai, Judaism survived.

A New Judaism Is Born

It was a new type of Judaism that survived. No longer was the Holy Temple the central focus of Judaism. Instead, Jews established places of prayer wherever they gathered. Previously, only priests—themselves the sons of priests—had conducted the religious ceremonies. Now any knowledgeable person could lead services, and the study of the Bible was the duty of all Jews. Jews would not rule in Jerusalem again for nearly 1,900 years. But as our people moved to new countries and eventually new continents, they were able to bring their modern religion with them. Because of Yoḥanan ben Zakkai's bravery and foresight, Judaism was able to continue to exist and flourish for thousands of years.

If you had been in Rabbi Yoḥanan's position, what would you have requested from Vespasian?

Eyewitness to History

The story of Yoḥanan ben Zakkai is found in the Talmud—a compilation of laws and legends that is based on the Torah and was written during the first five centuries of the common era. The story is probably part legend and part history. The section that follows, adapted from the Babylonian Talmud, Gittin 56, is perhaps the most dramatic story in the Talmud.

There were many zealots in Jerusalem.

The rabbis said to the zealots, "We must go out and make peace with the Romans."

The zealots refused and said to the contrary, "We must go out and fight them." Then the zealots went out and burned up all the wheat and barley that had been stored in order to create a famine, so that the people

A coin minted shortly after the fall of Jerusalem shows Judea (pictured as a woman) weeping under a palm tree as a Roman soldier stands over her. The inscription reads, "Judea Capta."

would be desperate and would fight the Romans.

Now the leader of the zealots in Jerusalem was named Abba Sikra. He was the nephew of Rabbi Yoḥanan ben Zakkai. The rabbi sent for his nephew, saying, "Come visit me secretly." When Abba Sikra arrived, his uncle Rabbi Yoḥanan turned to him and said, "How long are you going to carry on in this way and kill everybody by starving them?"

Abba Sikra replied, "What can I do? If I object, the other zealots will kill me."

Rabbi Yoḥanan then said, "Come up with a plan for me to escape from this city. Maybe I can still save something."

Abba Sikra thought of a scheme and replied, "Pretend to be very sick. Put something under you that smells awful, so that people will say that you have died and your corpse is rotting. When they are ready to carry you out, ask two of your closest disciples to hide underneath, so the people will think that the bier is heavy with a dead man."

Rabbi Yoḥanan did as he was told, but when they carried him out of the house in the bier, some men wanted to make sure he was dead by stabbing the bier. Abba Sikra said to them, "Do you want the Romans to see such a disrespectful act, stabbing your teacher?" Then they wanted to push and drop the bier. He said to them, "Do you want the Romans to see such a disrespectful act, pushing your teacher's bier?" So they went through the city's gate. And so Rabbi Yoḥanan escaped.

Rabbi Yoḥanan reached the Roman camp and was brought to the commanding general, Vespasian. He said to the general, "Peace to you, O king, peace to you, O king."

Vespasian replied, "You deserve to die for calling me king, because I am not the emperor." But just at that moment a messenger came to Vespasian and said, "Arise, for the emperor is dead, and you have been elected the new ruler!"

Vespasian turned and said to Rabbi Yoḥanan, "I am going now and will send someone to take my place. But you can make one request of me, and I will grant it."

Rabbi Yoḥanan said, "Give me Yavneh and its sages . . . so that we have a place to keep our heritage alive."

How did Rabbi Yoḥanan ben Zakkai sneak out of Jerusalem?

Exploring the Mitzvah

Talmud Torah

"The study of Torah is greater than all other deeds."

—Talmud, Peah 1:1, Shab.127a

Studying for your Bar or Bat Mitzvah, learning Hebrew, even reading this book all count as Talmud Torah.

Why does the Talmud consider the study of the Torah to be the most important mitzvah? Why did Rabbi Yoḥanan ben Zakkai risk his life for this mitzvah?

In the Talmud, we read that the study of Torah is greater than all other deeds "because it leads to them all." Torah is the accumulated wisdom of

What is the
most important
lesson you
have learned
from studying
Torah?

the Jewish people, acquired over more than 3,000 years. When we study our heritage, we learn about our values and our responsibilities. And we learn about the right way to act.

Studying Torah can help us make ethical decisions. Let's say you find a wallet in the street. Should you keep the money? What would you say if someone else found a wallet and asked you whether he or she should keep the money?

Are these simple questions?

Perhaps your answers would be different if you knew more about the situation. Was there a name in the wallet? Was the wallet found in a deserted area or in a particular store? Has anyone reported a lost wallet?

Each of these pieces of information affects the decision. So how do we know what is right? Is there a correct Jewish response?

Jews have been struggling with questions of right and wrong for over 3,000 years! We have been writing down our attempts to answer the questions of life, big and small, for almost as long. The Torah, Talmud, and Midrash all contain the Jewish people's search for answers.

Judaism teaches that the first step in deciding what is right is to study. Study your own tradition. Learn what it says. But don't stop there. First learn, then decide, then do!

In the case presented above, there is a whole section of Jewish law, halachah, concerned with the question of the wallet. It is called *avedah*, the rules of lost property. According to the Talmud, a person who comes across lost property of value must take it into his or her custody, care for it, and make an effort to find its rightful owner. That effort should include bringing the object to the notice of the public. Only after a determination that there is no reasonable chance of ever locating the original owner can the finder rightfully stake a claim.

The Bible, Talmud, and Midrash offer wise advice for the resolution of life's common problems. Can you think of other ethical questions? How might your knowledge of Jewish law and traditions help you resolve these problems?

Rabbi Yohanan ben Zakkai believed that the secret to the survival of the Jewish people was the commitment to Torah study. He believed that if the Jewish people had no guide to follow—no Torah—the will to survive would fail. Many Jews throughout the centuries have felt that it is loyalty to the Torah that has kept the Jews alive.

At your Bar or Bat Mitzvah ceremony, you read a portion from the Torah. By asking you to lead the service, the members of your synagogue and the rabbi show that they believe you are ready to understand our

LIVING THE MITZVAH

Read this week's Torah portion.

Find out what portion is being read by consulting a Jewish calendar or asking your teacher, principal, or rabbi. Read the portion in a translation of the Torah you have at home or in one you can borrow from the synagogue.

laws and traditions. By learning your Torah portion, you show that you are ready to begin accepting responsibility for your actions. You show that you are ready to begin making a commitment to doing mitzvot.

Talmud Torah, the study that comes before the doing, is a lifelong pursuit. It does not end at age twelve or thirteen; it is only the beginning! Every day of your life you will be called upon to make moral decisions. As a Jew, you are taught to respond not merely with what "feels" right but with what you have learned from the wisdom of your heritage.

Reading this book is an act of Talmud Torah. As the sage Hillel remarked, "So now, go and study!"

The more we study the Torah, the more we realize how necessary it is to perform mitzvot. The people in the photo on the left are fulfilling the mitzvah of Gemilut Ḥasadim (acts of kindness) by collecting reusable eyeglasses to send to needy people around the world. The boy at the right is fulfilling the mitzvah of Ma'achil R'evim (feeding the hungry) by packing gefilte fish, wine, and matzah to share with needy people in his community on Passover.

 # In Our Ancestors' Footsteps

The Ten Martyrs
Yoḥanan ben Zakkai risked his life so that the Torah would never be forgotten. But even after Yavneh was spared, the Romans continued to

make life difficult for Jews. They destroyed the Holy Temple in Jerusalem, forbade the teaching of Torah, and imposed the death sentence on any rabbi who ordained other rabbis.

For the next 100 years, a rabbi had to be brave as well as scholarly. Rabbis often taught their students in fields or forests so that they could escape quickly if Roman troops suddenly attacked. During the reign of Emperor Hadrian (117-138 C.E.) the Romans killed ten leading rabbis, including renowned scholars Rabbi Akiba and Rabbi Yehudah ben Bava.

We recall these and other martyrs during the afternoon Yom Kippur services. On the holiest day in the Jewish calendar, we remember our ancestral heroes who died for the sake of the Torah.

SPOTLIGHT ON THE BIBLE: EZRA

The first instance of studying the Torah can be found in the Bible itself. In the Book of Nehemiah, we read about the priest and scribe Ezra, who is credited with having been the first to write down the words of the Torah. To help Jews remember the teachings of the Torah, Ezra arranged to have the Torah read out loud. In a highly emotional scene, Ezra gathered the people of Jerusalem to listen to the words of the Torah. At first, they responded by weeping and prostrating themselves. But Ezra instructed them instead to celebrate, to sing and dance, to eat special meals, and to share what they had with the hungry.

> *And all the people gathered together into the square before the Water Gate; and they told Ezra the scribe to bring the book of the law of Moses which God had given to Israel. And Ezra the priest brought the Torah before the assembly, both men and women and all who could hear with understanding. . . . And the ears of all the people were attentive to the Torah. . . . And Ezra opened the book in the sight of all the people, for he was above all the people, and when he opened it all the people stood. . . . The Levites helped the people to understand the Torah, while the people remained in their places. And they read from the book, from the Law of God, clearly; and they gave the sense so that the people understood the reading.*
>
> (Nehemiah 8:1-8)

You Are There

Throughout history, oppressors of the Jews have tried to outlaw the study of the Torah. From the time of ancient Rome to the recent Soviet Union, Jews have risked torture and death for the rewards of studying the Bible and Talmud.

If you were one of the sages of Yavneh and had just heard of Rabbi Yoḥanan ben Zakkai's daring mission, how would you feel?

Not all the rabbis agreed with Rabbi Yoḥanan's request. Many rabbis felt that Rabbi Yoḥanan should have asked for the Jews to be spared death. Rabbi Yoḥanan thought, however, that such a great request would not be granted.

How does it make you feel to know of the sacrifices our ancestors made so that we can live freely and practice our religion today?

～ Jewish Heroes Hall of Fame ～

Turn to page 99, and read the introduction to the Jewish Heroes Hall of Fame. Afterward, complete page 100.

LIVING THE MITZVAH

Read a Jewish book, and add it to your personal library.

Ask your school or synagogue librarian to suggest a title. Do you want a reference book or a work of fiction? You might want to borrow a copy from the library before you decide to buy it.

2

K'LAL YISRAEL כְּלַל יִשְׂרָאֵל

THE MITZVAH OF JEWISH SOLIDARITY

"Israel is one, though dispersed among the seventy nations."
—ZOHAR, EXODUS 16:6

K'lal Yisrael means literally "all the people of Israel" and is the mitzvah of promoting Jewish unity. This mitzvah reminds Jews that they are responsible for one another no matter where they live or what they do. Pictured above is a rally in America to help free Soviet Jews.

A PITCHER GOES TO SYNAGOGUE

Time: October 1965

Place: Los Angeles, California

People: *Sandy Koufax*: star pitcher of the Los Angeles Dodgers;
Don Riley: sports columnist

In October 1965, the Los Angeles Dodgers faced the Minneapolis Twins in the World Series. Teams usually send their best pitcher out to start the first game of the World Series, and everyone knew that meant Sandy Koufax would be on the mound for the Dodgers.

At age 29, Sandy Koufax wasn't merely the best pitcher on his team. He threw the ball as well as any other pitcher who ever lived. He won the Cy

Sandy Koufax delivering a pitch during the World Series.

Young Award (given to the season's best pitcher) three times in four years; he was the first pitcher to throw four no-hitters. For the Dodgers to have any chance of defeating the Twins, they needed Koufax to pitch his best.

But as it turned out, the first game of the 1965 World Series fell on Yom Kippur. And Sandy Koufax was Jewish. Could the Dodgers count on Sandy Koufax to pitch that day?

Born and raised in Brooklyn, New York, Sandy Koufax grew up a die-hard sports fan. Talk-show host Larry King was a childhood friend of his; King remembers that Koufax's parents always took their children to synagogue on the High Holidays. In addition, they kept kosher and emphasized what King calls the "Jewish values" of family, loyalty, and helping the needy.

A Controversial Decision

In the first game of the World Series, Sandy Koufax was not on the field with his teammates. He was in synagogue with his fellow Jews, praying.

Koufax never expected his decision to be controversial. He did what he knew was the right thing; his manager and teammates supported him. But the day after the first game, a columnist for the *St. Paul Pioneer Press* wrote a column that many people considered anti-Semitic. (See Sandy Koufax's own description of the events in the Eyewitness to History section.) Suddenly, everyone was talking about the conflict of religion and sports.

Living Up to Your Potential

Why do you think some people were critical of Sandy Koufax for not pitching in the World Series?

As it turned out, the columnist for the St. Paul paper apologized for his remarks. Sandy Koufax pitched well in the second and fifth games of the World Series. Koufax then came back to pitch the seventh and deciding game after only two days' rest. He threw his second straight shutout as the Dodgers won one of the most dramatic World Series games in history. Two years later arm pain forced Koufax to retire at the young age of 31. Six years later he became the youngest player ever inducted into the Baseball Hall of Fame.

Sandy Koufax's simple decision to forgo a baseball game on Yom Kippur made a powerful impression on a generation of American Jews. To give you an idea of the impact of Koufax's decision, the writer Ze'ev Chafets reported twenty years later that in doing research for a book, "I was told by hundreds of Jewish men across the United States that their most important Jewish memory was of Sandy sitting out the Series."

Eyewitness to History

The following is an excerpt from *Koufax*, Sandy Koufax's autobiography. In this passage, Koufax recounts the events surrounding his decision not to pitch in the World Series and to attend Yom Kippur services instead.

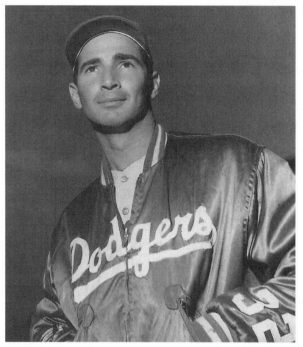

Sandy Koufax.

I had ducked a direct answer about the World Series because it seemed presumptuous to talk about it while we were still trying to get there. For all I knew, I could be home watching [it] on television.

I had tried to deflect questions about my intentions through the last couple of weeks of the season by saying that I was praying for rain.

There was never any decision to make, though, because there was never any possibility that I would pitch.

Yom Kippur is the holiest day of the Jewish religion. The club knows that I don't work that day.

The surprise of the day, as far as I was concerned, came the next morning when I was reading the report of the game by Don Riley, the columnist of the *St. Paul Pioneer Press*. His column took the form of "An Open Letter to Sandy Koufax," in which he was kind enough to tell me how

Why was Sandy Koufax convinced that he should not pitch in the World Series on Yom Kippur?

badly we had been beaten in the opener and warn me of the terrible things that lay in store for me.

I found it vastly amusing. Until right at the end. "And the Twins love matzoh balls on Thursdays."

I couldn't believe it. I thought that kind of thing went out with dialect comics.

I clipped the column so that I could send it back to him after we defeated the Twins with a friendly little notation that I hoped his words were as easy to eat as my matzoh balls.

I didn't, of course. We were winners. The winners laugh, drink champagne, and give the losers the benefit of all doubts.

Exploring the Mitzvah

K'lal Yisrael

One of the reasons it's a mitzvah for Jews to feel responsible for one another is simply that the Jewish people have never been large in numbers. Even today there are about six million Jews in the United States, out of a total population of about 250 million.

In order to practice K'lal Yisrael, it is necessary to understand the needs of other Jews.

Do a quick division. In the United States, the Jews are less than 2.5 percent of the population!

In the entire world there are 5.6 billion people, of which, 18 million are Jews. That means only 0.32 percent of the world's population is Jewish!

Size is certainly one factor contributing to the importance placed on the mitzvah of promoting closeness among Jews. In this regard, wanting future generations to be Jewish means doing your part to care for the Jewish community, to ensure that it will be around for centuries to come.

Shared history is another reason for working on behalf of K'lal Yisrael. Any group of people who have gone through the intense experiences of joy and sorrow together are likely to feel special bonds. And Jews have gone through incredible experiences together. In this century alone, think about the sorrows and joys Jews have experienced as a people. *With the help of your parents or teachers, list three of each.*

A third reason Jews feel responsible for one another is that the Jewish tradition teaches that it is the right thing to do. The Torah teaches that we should care for all people, even the stranger in our midst. How much more so those with whom we have a special bond! Often you may hear Jews say: if we do not take care of our own, who will? That is why almost every Jewish community has institutions that take care of Jews in need. *With the help of your parents or teachers, think of three such places.*

For all these reasons, working for K'lal Yisrael is a mitzvah. Sandy Koufax knew that to pitch on Yom Kippur would compromise his religious beliefs. And he knew that if he did pitch, he would be sending the wrong message about the Jewish people. In standing up for his beliefs, Sandy Koufax exemplified these words of the Mishnah: "All Jews are responsible for one another."

In Our Ancestors' Footsteps

The Jewish Olympics

Many of the greatest Jewish athletes of modern times compete in the Maccabiah Games, which have been called the "Jewish Olympics." Held every four years, the Maccabiah Games are open to Jewish athletes from all over the world. The tournament was created, in part, to instill Jewish pride and unity among young Jews throughout the world. The first games were held in 1932 in Tel Aviv; 390 athletes from 14 countries

Mark Spitz carries the torch on his way to lighting the flame to signal the opening of the 12th Maccabiah Games.

participated. In 1993, over 5,000 athletes from 50 countries came to compete. In 1969, a young swimmer named Mark Spitz first won fame at the Maccabiah Games. A few years later, in 1972, he won a record seven gold medals at the Olympic Games.

SPOTLIGHT ON THE BIBLE: ESTHER

Many Jews in the Bible have performed the mitzvah of K'lal Yisrael. Perhaps the best example is Esther, who risked her life on behalf of the Jewish people. *Can you think of another person in the Bible whose actions reflect a passion for K'lal Yisrael?*

You Are There

LIVING THE MITZVAH

Explore the Jewish groups on the Internet.

With the help of any on-line friend, do a search of all the different Jewish Web sites, and see just how diverse the Jewish world is.

You are an actor in a school play that is scheduled to have its opening night on the first night of Passover.

The other actors in the play tell you that no one else could do the role as well as you. They ask you not to let them down. Your teacher, who is not Jewish, questions how important Passover really is. A friend suggests you go to the seder with your parents but then leave early in order to arrive at school in time for the play.

What do you do? How do you arrive at your solution?

⟶ *Jewish Heroes Hall of Fame* ⟵

Complete page 101 in the Jewish Heroes Hall of Fame.

3

TZIONUT צִיּוֹנוּת

THE MITZVAH OF ZIONISM

"Zionism is the return of the Jews to Judaism, before their return to the Jewish land." —THEODOR HERZL
(ADDRESS TO THE FIRST ZIONIST CONGRESS, AUGUST 29, 1897)

Tzionut is the mitzvah of Zionism, supporting Israel. Tzion (Zion) is an ancient name for the land of Israel. For over 1,800 years, Jews never lost their feeling of attachment to their ancestral homeland and never gave up the hope of rebuilding a Jewish state. Now that Israel is a reality, the mitzvah of Tzionut means that we must help Israel no matter where we live. Pictured here is a Los Angeles celebration—Solidarity Day with Israel.

The Jews Of Silence No More

Time: Rosh Hashanah, October 4, 1948
Place: The Great Synagogue, Moscow, Russia
People: *Golda Meir*: newly appointed Israeli minister to the Soviet Union;
Ilya Ehrenburg: an influential newspaper columnist;
50,000 Russian Jews

Golda Meir was born in Russia in 1898. Anti-Semitism flourished in those times, and many Jews left Russia to seek better places to live. When Golda was eight years old, she and her parents emigrated to the United States. Golda grew up in Milwaukee, Wisconsin, and became a school-teacher. She developed a passion for Zionism as a teenager, and in 1921 she and her husband made the brave decision to emigrate to Palestine. She held several important positions in the labor movement there, and shortly after Israel declared independence, Meir was given the great responsibility of serving as Israel's minister to the Soviet Union.

For approximately 70 years of Communist rule, Jews and other religious groups in Russia were not free to practice their faith. The St. Petersburg synagogue, below, is evidence of the well-established Jewish community of pre-Communist days.

Golda Meir, later to become Prime Minister of Israel, was surrounded by an excited crowd of Jews outside the Great Synagogue in Moscow.

In 1948, more than 3 million Jews lived in the Soviet Union—five times the number of Jews who lived in Israel. The Russian Revolution of 1917 had trapped them—no one was allowed to leave the country. Anti-Semitism continued to thrive, and the Communists instituted laws preventing religious services and religious education. Jews could not freely attend synagogue services, learn Hebrew, or study Torah.

Golda knew the Soviets would try to keep her away from meeting and talking with the local Jewish population. "I desperately wanted to make contact with . . . the Jews of Russia, from whom we had been separated for thirty years—since the Revolution—and about whom we knew almost nothing," Golda confided years later. "What were they like? What had remained of their Jewishness after so many years?"

Moscow's Jews were warned to stay away from the Israeli delegation. In a long essay in *Pravda*, an official Soviet newspaper, Ilya Ehrenburg wrote that "the State of Israel has nothing to do with the Jews of the Soviet Union, where there is no Jewish problem and therefore no need for Israel."

Punishment Without Crime

Jews who disobeyed the Soviet authorities risked being sent to Siberia (the vast cold region where numerous prison camps were built). Members of Golda's delegation who had close relatives in Moscow "were in an agony of doubt . . . as to whether or not they should contact people whom they longed to see, but whom they knew might be condemned to deportation if their relationship with any Israeli were to be revealed."

On Rosh Hashanah, Golda attended services at Moscow's Great Synagogue. Despite its name, usually only 100 elderly Jewish men attended Shabbat services there. When she arrived at the synagogue, she was astonished to see the street packed with people.

Why was it dangerous to be a practicing Jew in Communist Russia?

For the Jews of Moscow, turning out to attend Rosh Hashanah services with Golda Meir was a way for them to express their excitement about the establishment of Israel and to support Israel's representatives in Russia.

Thank You for Having Remained Jews

As she left the Great Synagogue, Golda called out in Yiddish, "Thank you for having remained Jews." That sentence was repeated thousands of times throughout the crowd; in the following weeks, the words spread throughout the country. As Golda Meir's son later recalled, "The Jews of Russia had awakened and their long silence was about to be broken."

Golda went on to become prime minister of Israel and one of the most beloved figures in world politics. In their act of of bravery, the Jews of

Moscow had shown their dictator, Joseph Stalin, that they remained committed to their faith, regardless of the oppression they faced. Though it took several more decades and uncountable acts of heroism, eventually Russia allowed its Jews to emigrate to Israel—and more than 700,000 of them leaped at the opportunity.

Eyewitness to History

This account of Golda Meir's Rosh Hashanah visit to the Moscow synagogue is from her autobiography, *My Life*. The book was a national best-seller in America when it was published in 1975.

Golda Meir.

As we had planned, we went to the synagogue on Rosh Hashanah. All of us—the men, women and children of the delegation—dressed in our best clothes, as befitted Jews on a Jewish holiday. But the street in front of the synagogue had changed. Now it was filled with people, packed together like sardines, hundreds and hundreds of them, of all ages, including Red Army officers, soldiers, teenagers and babies carried in their parents' arms. Instead of the 2,000-odd Jews who usually came to the synagogue on the holidays, a crowd of close to 50,000 people was waiting for us. For a minute I couldn't grasp what had happened—or even who they were. And then it dawned on me. They had come—those good, brave Jews—in order to be with us, to demonstrate their sense of kinship and to celebrate the establishment of the State of Israel. Within seconds, they had surrounded me, almost lifting me bodily, almost crushing me, saying my name over and over again. Eventually, they parted ranks and let me enter the synagogue, but there, too, the demonstration went on. Every now and then, in the women's gallery, someone would come to me, touch my hand, stroke or even kiss my dress. Without speeches or parades, without any words at all really, the Jews of Moscow were proving their profound desire—and their need—to participate in the miracle of the establishment of the Jewish state, and I was the symbol of the state for them.

I couldn't talk, or smile, or wave my hand. I sat in that gallery like a stone, without moving, with those thousands of eyes fixed on me. No such entity as the Jewish people, Ehrenburg had written. The State of Israel meant nothing to the Jews of the USSR! But his warning had fallen

Why did the Soviet Jews come by the thousands to see Golda Meir?

on deaf ears. For thirty years we and they had been separated. Now we were together again, and as I watched them, I knew that no threat, however awful, could possibly have stopped the ecstatic people I saw in the synagogue that day from telling us, in their own way, what Israel meant to them. The service ended, and I got up to leave; but I could hardly walk. I felt as though I had been caught up in a torrent of love so strong that it had literally taken my breath away and slowed down my heart. I was on the verge of fainting, I think. But the crowd still surged around me, stretching out its hands and saying *Nasha Golda* (our Golda) and *shalom, shalom*, and crying.

Exploring the Mitzvah

Tzionut
"Zionism is an idea, a necessity, a moving force in the lives of all Jews."
—JUDAH MAGNES

David Ben-Gurion reading the Israeli Declaration of Independence in 1948.

Why is helping Israel a mitzvah for all Jews? In part, the answer to this question is connected to another mitzvah we have studied, K'lal Yisrael. If all Jews are responsible for one another, then certainly that responsibility extends to the Jews of Israel. Soon after the modern state of Israel was born, the World Zionist Congress defined the "task of Zionism" in a way that highlights Zionism as an expression of K'lal Yisrael. According to the resolution, Zionism is:

1. the strengthening of the State of Israel
2. the ingathering of exiles in the Land of Israel
3. the fostering of the unity of the Jewish people

(Resolution, August 29, 1951)

When Golda Meir was prime minister, she pointed out that Zionism and Israel now meant that there was no such thing as a Jewish refugee any longer. "The Jewish state," she declared, "is prepared to take every Jew, whether he has anything or not, whether he is a skilled worker or not, whether he is sick or not. It doesn't make a particle of difference."

Zionism is a way of helping the Jews of Israel, but it is more. It is also a way of thinking about the Jewish people and Judaism. For many Zionists, Israel is the center of Jewish renewal, a place that inspires them to learn about Jewish history, culture, and their own Jewish identity. Golda Meir once remarked that "every mountain, every valley in our country tells of our belonging, of our being here. This is where we were for thousands of years, this is where we belong. . . . We are not a new people. We have not come back to a new country. We are an old people that has come back to its old home."

There are a number of ways we can observe the mitzvah of Zionism. These include:

1. visiting Israel
2. contributing money to Israeli charities
3. learning Hebrew
4. studying about Israel

Which of these have you done? Can you think of other ways of observing this mitzvah?

In Our Ancestors' Footsteps

Judah HaLevi, an Early Zionist

Centuries before there was a modern State of Israel or an organized Zionist movement, Jews continually dreamed about and prayed for the reestablishment of their homeland. One of the greatest examples of Tzionut was Judah HaLevi. Born in Spain shortly before the year 1075, HaLevi made his living as a physician and a merchant. He was active in community affairs and also was a philosopher. One of his works, *The*

LIVING THE MITZVAH

Start saving for a trip to Israel.

A visit to Israel before high school graduation is a wonderful experience. Perhaps you could set aside gift money from your Bar or Bat Mitzvah celebration. Speak to your parents about this, and find out from your synagogue or community center about trips to Israel for high school students.

A page from The Kuzari by Judah HaLevi.

LIVING THE MITZVAH

Get an Israeli pen pal.

Your religious school principal can help make a match. Another possibility is to find out if you have any extended family living in Israel, and ask them if there is anyone your age interested in corresponding. You could then visit that person when you are in Israel.

Kuzari, is still studied today.

But Judah HaLevi is best remembered for his magnificent poetry. The most famous of these poems are his "Songs of Zion," which speak of his overwhelming desire to live in the Holy Land. One poem begins with lines that have become an enduring classic of Hebrew literature:

> My heart is in the East and I am at the edge of the West. Then how can I taste what I eat, how can I enjoy it? How can I fulfill my vows and pledges while Zion is [captive]? It would be easy for me to leave all the good things of Spain; it would be glorious to see the dust of the ruined Temple.

Judah HaLevi not only wrote about his deep Zionist feelings, he actually attempted the perilous journey to the Holy Land in 1140, knowing that if he managed to reach it, harsh living conditions awaited him. HaLevi made it as far as Alexandria, Egypt, a major Jewish community. After a stopover, he boarded a ship to Palestine, but its departure was delayed because of bad weather. HaLevi died before the ship set sail again.

SPOTLIGHT ON THE BIBLE: PSALMS

The Jewish people's love of Israel can be found throughout the Bible. Many of the most beautiful passages reflecting our people's love for Israel were written after the Jews had been exiled from their homeland. The following section is from Psalm 137. It describes the emotions of Jews who were forced to leave Israel and live in Babylon, over 2,500 years ago.

By the waters of Babylon, there we sat down and wept, when we remembered Zion. On the willows there we hung up our lyres. For there our captors required of us songs, and our tormentors, mirth, saying, 'Sing us one of the songs of Zion!'

How can we sing God's song in a foreign land? If I forget you, O Jerusalem, let my right hand wither! Let my tongue cleave to the roof of my mouth, if I do not remember you, if I do not set Jerusalem above my highest joy!

You Are There

Imagine you were the chief rabbi of Moscow's Great Synagogue in 1948. It's Rosh Hashanah and Golda Meir has arrived. You start the services and look out to see more people in the synagogue than you've ever seen before. Many of them are Jews who have never been to Rosh Hashanah services before. Some of them are presumably Russian secret police.

What is the topic of your sermon? What would you want to say so that everyone would feel included in your thoughts?

~ Jewish Heroes Hall of Fame ~

Complete page 102 in the Jewish Heroes Hall of Fame.

---

4 TIKKUN OLAM תִּקּוּן עוֹלָם

THE MITZVAH OF HEALING THE WORLD

"Some are guilty; all are responsible."
—ABRAHAM JOSHUA HESCHEL

Tikkun Olam is the mitzvah of social action. The Hebrew word *tikkun* means to "fix" or "heal" something that is broken; *olam* means "world." Tikkun Olam refers to all actions that benefit our society, and it includes all work that helps our local community as well as the deeds that aid the planet as a whole.

SOME ARE GUILTY, ALL ARE RESPONSIBLE

Setting the Scene ✴ ✴ ✴ ✴ ✴

Time: 1963, 1965

Place: Selma, Alabama

People: *Abraham Joshua Heschel*: rabbi, scholar, philosopher, and social activist;

Martin Luther King, Jr.: Baptist minister and pioneering leader of the civil rights movement

Abraham Joshua Heschel had a firsthand knowledge of what injustice means. Born in Poland, Heschel was forced to flee the Nazis. He reached the United States in 1940 and became a professor, first at Hebrew Union College and later at the Jewish Theological Seminary. As a teacher, philosopher, and prolific author, Heschel influenced a generation of rabbis, educators, and lay people.

Abraham Joshua Heschel (second from right, front) marching with Martin Luther King, Jr. (fourth from right, front) in a civil rights march in Alabama.

One of Heschel's most important works was a 1962 book entitled *The Prophets*. In it, he analyzed the prophets of the Bible and compared their messages to those of the philosophers and prophets of other religions. Shortly before his death, he made a revealing statement in a TV interview:

> I've written a book on the prophets on which I spent many years. And really this book changed my life. Because early in my life, my great love was for learning, studying. And the place where I preferred to live was my study and books and writing and thinking. I've learned from the prophets that I have to be involved in the affairs of man, in the affairs of suffering man.

For Heschel, this meant he needed to become involved in the great social issues of his day. The 1960s have become known as a decade of dissent, but protests were far rarer in the early 1960s than in the late 1960s. Heschel's involvement in numerous protests during the early 1960s helped lead the way for others to join in.

Heschel was among the first to protest against the Vietnam War. He also played an important, behind-the-scenes role in working with the Vatican to reevaluate Catholicism's relationship with Judaism. In addition, Heschel joined with the Reverend Martin Luther King, Jr. in protesting against the lack of civil rights for blacks in the United States.

Martin Luther King, Jr. was a proponent of nonviolent civil disobedience. He first gained national attention in 1956 by leading a bus strike in Birmingham, Alabama. A riveting speaker and inspired leader, he convinced people of all political and religious backgrounds to join with him to protest against the unfair laws and treatment blacks received. With King's leadership, the plight of blacks in America improved dramatically. Eventually King was awarded the Nobel Peace Prize. King himself credited Heschel's stirring address to the Conference on Religion and Race in Chicago in 1963 with motivating clergy of all faiths to join the civil rights movement.

A New Way to Pray

One of the most famous protests in the civil rights movement was held in Selma, Alabama, in 1965. Although Congress had passed a law the previous year upholding blacks' right to vote, local authorities, including the police, were doing their utmost to make sure the law was not carried out. King organized a peaceful march to show the world how blacks were being mistreated.

Heschel's decision to march with King was widely heralded. After the protest march, Heschel (who was a master at coining striking phrases) declared, "When I marched in Selma, my feet were praying."

What motivated Heschel to become a social activist?

Throughout Heschel's life, he never lost sight of his passion for improving the world. In writing about why he was protesting the Vietnam War, Heschel said, "We must continue to remind ourselves that in a free society, all are involved in what some are doing. Some are guilty, all are responsible."

Eyewitness to History

Below are excerpts from various books by Rabbi Abraham Joshua Heschel.

Abraham Joshua Heschel.

Prayer is meaningless unless it . . . seeks to overthrow and to ruin the pyramids of callousness, hatred, opportunism, falsehood. The liturgical movement must become a revolutionary movement, seeking to overthrow the forces that continue to destroy the promise, the hope, the vision.

As surely as we are driven to live, we are driven to serve spiritual ends that surpass our own interests. "The good drive" is not invented by society but is something which makes society possible; not an accidental function but of the very essence of man. We may lack a clear perception of its meaning, but we are moved by the horror of its violation. . . . Mitzvot are spiritual ends.

The meaning of man's life lies in his perfecting the universe. He has to distinguish, gather, and redeem the sparks of holiness scattered throughout the darkness of the world. This service is the motive of all precepts and good deeds.

What does Heschel mean when he writes, "The meaning of man's life is in his perfecting the universe"?

How can you help "perfect the universe"?

What drove me to study the prophets? In the academic environment in which I spent my student years philosophy had become an isolated, self-subsisting, self-indulgent entity, encouraging suspicion instead of love of wisdom. The answers offered were unrelated to the problems, indifferent to the travail of a person who became aware of man's suspended sensitivity in the face of stupendous challenge. . . .

The prophet was an individual who said "No" to his society, condemning its habits and assumptions. . . . He [the prophet] was often compelled to proclaim the very opposite of what his heart expected. His fundamental objective was to reconcile man and God.

Exploring the Mitzvah

Tikkun Olam

"May we soon behold . . . the repair of the world." —SIDDUR

A leading Jewish periodical in the United States is called *Tikkun*. The magazine explains the meaning of its title on the back cover:

"Tikkun (te-kun) . . . to heal, repair and transform the world."

LIVING THE MITZVAH

Conserve natural resources.

Discuss with your parents one opportunity for making your home ecologically fit. Offer to take charge of making that change happen. In addition to recycling paper and glass, you might want to think about installing energy-saving light bulbs, low-flow shower heads, or upgrading the insulation in your home.

Cleaning up the environment is one way to practice Tikkun Olam.

The mitzvah of Tikkun Olam refers to making the world a better place. Tikkun Olam is based on the premise that we *can* make a difference in the world, and we *should* make a difference in the world! It is based on the conviction, in Heschel's words, that "By whatever we do, by every act we carry out, we either advance or obstruct the drama of redemption; we either reduce or enhance the power of evil."

As Heschel pointed out, the call to better the world is an ancient call in Judaism. The great biblical prophets, such as Isaiah and Jeremiah, insisted that Jews become involved in the moral problems of the day.

Later the medieval mystics of Judaism spoke of the world as broken and fragmented. They described sparks of God's light that have become scattered throughout the universe. The mystics claimed that our purpose in life is to help God collect the sparks again. In doing so, we not only help repair the world, but move humanity one step closer to redemption—the time when goodness will fully prevail over evil.

How can our world be described as "broken," and in what ways can it be healed?

In our time, the imagery of Tikkun Olam has led to its adoption as the Hebrew term for "social action." Fulfilling the responsibility of Tikkun Olam means not isolation from, but activity in, the community. Many synagogues have a social action committee; some are even called Tikkun Olam committees.

In Our Ancestors' Footsteps

Rose Schneiderman

Whether campaigning to improve working conditions in garment factories or securing women's suffrage, Rose Schneiderman fought for the rights of all women.

Performing the act of Tikkum Olam requires not only speaking out against the wrongdoings of others, but also taking action to improve the world. Rose Schneiderman (1882-1972) did both.

When Rose Schneiderman was a young girl, there were few decent jobs for immigrants arriving in America. As a result, many immigrant women had no choice but to work in hot, overcrowded sweatshops, where they sat bent over sewing machines for twelve to fourteen hours a day, earning very little money.

Although women made up more than 70 percent of the labor force in the garment industry, there had been no active effort to organize these workers into a union. Rose Schneiderman would change all that. Schneiderman believed that workers could improve their situation if they banded together and spoke out as one. Schneiderman co-founded the first union of female workers in the garment industry and was the first woman elected to a leadership position in the trade union movement.

Although no more than four and a half feet tall, Schneiderman was a forceful presence. Throughout her life, Rose Schneiderman continued to fight for the rights of working women. She fought for minimum wages, equal pay for equal work, unemployment insurance, and safety in the workplace. When Schneiderman died in 1972, *The New York Times* wrote that she "did more to upgrade the dignity and living standards of working women than any other woman."

SPOTLIGHT ON THE BIBLE: PROPHETS

The prophets were our greatest voices speaking out for the betterment of humanity. They demanded that the Jewish people be held accountable for their moral behavior. They demanded that people reach beyond themselves and work for the common good.

The prophet Isaiah urged the Israelites to be "a light to the nations." He talked of an eventual era of universal peace and justice, envisioning a time when "My House shall be called a House of prayer for all peoples."

The prophet Amos cautioned that God hates those who do not do justice:

> *Even though you offer me your burnt offerings and cereal offerings, I will not accept them, and the peace offerings of your fatted beasts I will not look upon. . . . But let justice roll down like waters, and righteousness like an ever-flowing stream.*

The prophet Micah sounded the same chord:

> *Arise, plead your case before the mountains, and let the hills hear your voice. . . . God has showed you what is good; and what does Adonai require of you but to do justice, and to love kindness, and to walk humbly with your God.*

You Are There

Many campaigns are currently being waged in order to improve the world. Look at the list below. Which of these causes seem to you worthy of being called Tikkun Olam? Explain your choices.

1. The environmental movement
2. The anti-nuclear movement
3. The Anti-Defamation League
4. Recycling
5. Society for the Prevention of Cruelty to Animals

~ Jewish Heroes Hall of Fame ~

Complete pages 103 and 104 in the Jewish Heroes Hall of Fame.

LIVING THE MITZVAH

Become involved in a social action project.

Find out what social action projects are taking place at your synagogue or your school. (For example, housing the homeless once a month at the synagogue or collecting food for the hungry.) Choose a project for the year, and then pick a different one for next year.

5 OMETZ LEV אֹמֶץ לֵב

THE MITZVAH OF COURAGE

"Courage is never to let your actions be influenced by your fears."
—ARTHUR KOESTLER, ARROW IN THE BLUE

Ometz Lev is the mitzvah of courage. Ometz Lev literally means "dedication of the heart." When we fully set our heart on doing something, our determination can give us the inner strength to overcome fear, doubt, and other obstacles in our path.

A Sense Of Mission

Setting the Scene ✻ ✻ ✻ ✻ ✻

Time: March-November, 1944
Place: Behind enemy lines, in Nazi-occupied Yugoslavia and Hungary
People: *Hannah Senesh*: a 23-year-old kibbutznik;
Reuven Dafne and Yoel Palgi: paratroopers who accompanied
Senesh on her mission

Hannah Senesh was born in Budapest, Hungary, in 1921. Her father was a writer, and from an early age Hannah showed that she too was a gifted writer and poet.

As a teenager, Hannah became very involved in Zionist activity. In 1939, sickened by the anti-Semitism that filled Hungary, Hannah moved to Palestine. She joined a kibbutz and continued to write poetry.

That same year, World War II erupted, and the Hungarian government chose to side with Nazi Germany. Senesh could not stop thinking about

Hannah Senesh with her mother and brother George.

Allied soldiers parachuting behind enemy lines.

all her family and friends who were left behind in Budapest. In 1943, she joined the Palmach, the Jewish army in Palestine. She learned navigation, wireless radio transmitting, and parachuting.

The Palmach desperately wanted to help defeat the Nazis, and it also wanted to prove to the Allies (France, Great Britain, the United States, and the Soviet Union) that it could be useful in the war effort. It planned a daring raid to rescue prisoners of war and help Jews escape from the Nazis. The raid would be dangerous: it involved dropping commandos behind enemy lines.

Senesh volunteered for the raid. Besides her useful military skills, she also spoke fluent Hungarian. Privately, she hoped to rescue her mother, who was trapped in Budapest.

Senesh was the only woman chosen to go on the raid.

The day before Hannah Senesh set out on the mission, she wrote a letter to her brother that reveals the strength of her conviction:

> Day after tomorrow I am starting something new. . . . Perhaps it's dangerous. Perhaps one in a hundred—or one in a thousand, pays with his life.

> I wonder, will you understand? I wonder, will you believe that it is more than a childish wish for adventure, more than youthful romanticism that attracted me? I wonder, will you feel that I could not do otherwise, that this was something I had to do?

> There are events without which one's life becomes unimportant, a worthless toy; and there are times when one is commanded to do something, even at the price of one's life. (December 25, 1943)

In Nazi Hands

Senesh and her team parachuted from a plane and landed safely in Yugoslavia. A select group, including Senesh, proceeded to the Hungarian border. Soon thereafter Senesh was captured. The Gestapo tortured her in a Budapest prison, demanding to learn military secrets, including her radio code, that would have harmed the Allies.

The Gestapo brought Hannah's mother to the prison. They threatened to harm her if Hannah did not cooperate. Hannah refused to speak. She was sentenced to death and executed by a firing squad.

Word of Senesh's daring and strength spread throughout the Jews of Palestine, giving these settlers renewed determination in their own struggle to establish a Jewish state. In time, her diary and poems became well-known in Israel and the Jewish world, and a number of books about her life were published. Senesh's story was made into a motion picture (*Hannah's War*) in the 1980s.

Why did Hannah Senesh volunteer for such a dangerous mission?

In one of her diary entries at the beginning of the war Senesh wrote about why she was willing to face the danger of becoming a soldier to fight the Nazis:

> I'm not afraid for my life. It's dear to me, but there are things I hold more dear.

> Who and what am I to assume such a task? I can't do this, of course. But to do nothing, merely to look on from afar—that I can't do either.

> I want to believe catastrophe won't come to pass. But if it does, I hope we'll face it with honor. And if we can't hold out, then we will fall honorably.

Eyewitness to History

These testimonies were given by Hannah Senesh's fellow paratroopers, Reuven Dafne and Yoel Palgi.

Hannah Senesh.

She was fearless, and none of us was as positive as she that our mission would succeed. Never once did she consider the possibility of failure; never once did she allow us to become dispirited or discouraged. She would explain with iron logic how we could extricate ourselves from any predicament, and her inner conviction would reassure us. Of course she experienced moments of discouragement, but renewed strength constantly welled from the depths of her being.

When on the night of March 13, 1944, we were told to get ready to leave, she was overjoyed. She sang the whole way back to the village where we were quartered, and made us sing along with her. That song, in the course of our mission, became our group's theme song.

We sat inside the crowded plane, parcels all around us, some for the partisans, some for our own needs. We felt weighed down. What with the harness on our backs, the weapons, and our heavy winter clothes, we had almost no freedom of movement at all.

The thunderous roaring of the engines killed conversation. I studied the faces of my comrades, all deep in thought, and felt our hearts must be pounding in fateful unison. My eyes rested on Hannah. Her face was aglow, and she exuded happiness and excitement. She winked at me, waved her hand encouragingly, and a delightful, impish smile enveloped her features. . . . Her excitement was contagious; we were all infected by it. Gradually tension relaxed, and the air seemed lighter. Fears and black thoughts receded, finally disappeared, and we began feeling peacefully confident.

In what ways was Hannah Senesh a courageous person?

Four of us were lying alone, cut off in a thick forest, hidden behind tree trunks, our guns aimed. Our nerves were at the breaking point. . . . There were moments when we thought we would be unable to hold out another instant, but we plodded on, praying for a miracle. . . . I'll never forget Hannah's amazing composure. I would glance at her from time to time, lying there, pistol cocked, a heavenly radiance on her face. I was literally overwhelmed by wonder for this unique girl. Her remarkable strength of character, her courage, her integrity and unwavering dedication to our mission aroused my utmost admiration and respect.

Her behavior before members of the Gestapo and SS was quite remarkable. She always stood up to them, warning them plainly of the bitter fate they would suffer after their defeat. Curiously, these wild animals, in whom every spark of humanity had been extinguished, felt awed in the presence of this refined, fearless young girl. . . . Having been taught for years that Jews never fight back, that they will accept the vilest treatment, they were taken aback by her courage.

She suffered dreadful tortures, and she didn't want to talk about them. . . . I heard from others how they had tied her; how they had whipped her palms and the soles of her feet; bound her and forced her to sit motionless for hours on end; beaten her all over the body until she was black and blue. They asked her one thing, only one thing: what is your radio code? . . . Hannah was perfectly aware of the value of her code, and she didn't reveal it.

Exploring the Mitzvah

Ometz Lev
In Pirkei Avot (Sayings of the Fathers), we read an ages-old definition that still has meaning today: "Who is a hero? The person who overcomes one's bad side."

Our sages taught that every person has two inclinations: one toward the good and one toward the evil. We have the ability to choose between the two. Life is a continual struggle to enable our good intentions to prevail over our baser instincts.

Early Israeli pioneers had the courage to leave their old homes and try to build a new home in an often desolate area.

LIVING THE MITZVAH

Act courageously!

Discuss with your parents moments of courage that they remember in their lives. Then think about your own life. Is there a situation in which you could take a stand on an issue you know may be unpopular but is right? Is there a situation in which you realize that you were wrong, and still need to admit it? Taking action on either of these issues would be a personally courageous act.

Isn't it true that we all have to work at showing our "good side"? Being the best we can be is not always easy or fun. We all find ourselves in situations that call for us to stick our neck out, to take a risk for the sake of others. Sometimes we will choose the wrong side, or we will simply do nothing. Not everyone is brave, yet we all have the potential to display courage. It takes real dedication to be courageous in the face of risk or outright danger.

Hannah wrote in her diary, "If we close our eyes and listen only to our hearts, we hear the pounding of fear." She asked, "Who, and what am I, to assume such a task?" Was Hannah afraid? Yes. Did Hannah have doubts? Yes. Hannah was, however, strong enough to overcome her fears and self-doubt, and even to risk her life, because she believed so strongly in coming to the aid of her people. To her brother she wrote, "There are times when one is commanded to do something, even at the price of one's life."

How can an ordinary person in ordinary circumstances be brave?

As the sages taught, being heroic is not restricted to great people in great situations. As the cowardly lion in *The Wizard of Oz* learned, the potential for bravery is in us all the time, but we must search for it. The first step in our quest for courage is to be brave enough to confront ourselves.

When Moses was about to die, he summoned his successor, Joshua, to his side and charged him to be "strong and brave" (Deuteronomy 31:23). According to the Torah, God repeats these same words when speaking to Joshua later in his life (Joshua 1:6,9). Today, more than 30 centuries after Moses and Joshua, when people are about to set out on a difficult path, we still say to them, "*ḥazak v'ematz*—be strong and be brave!"

Stop and think for a moment about a very important question. What in your own life is most precious to you? Is anything so precious that you would be willing to risk your own safety and well-being to preserve it?

Do you wish you had more things about which to care, or fewer things?

In Our Ancestors' Footsteps

Hannah's Poems
From reading about the life of Hannah Senesh, we learn about her strength of character. She also exhibited her character and great depth of emotion in her poetry. Below are two of her poems.

Hannah Senesh together for the last time with her brother George.

Blessed Is the Match

Blessed is the match consumed
   in kindling flame.
Blessed is the flame that burns
   in the secret places of the heart.
Blessed is the heart with strength to stop
   its beating for honor's sake.
Blessed is the match consumed
   in kindling flame.

To a Good Friend

I wounded another not knowing
Both ends of an arrow mar.
I too was hurt in the battle
And shall bear a scar.

SPOTLIGHT ON THE BIBLE: JOSHUA

When we speak of courage in the Bible, Joshua comes to mind. Joshua proves his strength and determination in a dramatic display of courage during the Children of Israel's long trek in the desert, after they have been freed from Egyptian slavery.

In Numbers 13-14, Moses selects twelve men to scout out the Land of Israel. After forty days, the men return with a report that although Canaan is fertile ("a land of milk and honey"), it is inhabited by powerful people in fortified cities. Ten of the men claim there is no way the Israelites can enter the Promised Land. Their words touch off a near riot within the community. But Joshua and Caleb refuse to succumb to the mob's demand that Moses and Aaron be stripped of power and that the Israelites return to Egypt. They insist that the Israelites can move forward to the Promised Land. They plead their case that the people must have faith in themselves and in God.

Joshua displays the courage to stand up for his convictions and pursue what others think impossible. He goes on to lead the Israelites into Canaan with a series of daring military exploits. His personal bravery inspires his troops and encourages the people.

Can you think of other examples of Ometz Lev in the Bible?

 ## You Are There

You see some bullies picking on the new student in school, one who doesn't speak much English. If you go to the defense of the new student, the bullies might harass you, they might even attack you. You can think of any number of reasons not to get involved.

Are you brave enough to face the bullies? Does thinking about this question make you admire Hannah Senesh's bravery more?

⟶ *Jewish Heroes Hall of Fame* ⟵

Complete page 105 in the Jewish Heroes Hall of Fame.

ḤERUT   חֵרוּת

THE MITZVAH OF FREEDOM

"Next year in Jerusalem." —PASSOVER HAGGADAH

Ḥerut is the mitzvah of seeking freedom. Beginning with the Israelites' escape from slavery in Egypt more than 3,000 years ago, the struggle for freedom has been of crucial significance in Jewish history. This struggle has involved the fight for political freedom for ancient and modern Israel and for religious freedom wherever Jews have lived. Pictured above are Russian immigrants being greeted by relatives upon their arrival in Israel in 1993.

NEXT YEAR IN JERUSALEM

Setting the Scene ✦ ✦ ✦ ✦ ✦

Time: 1977 - 1986

Place: Moscow, Russia

People: *Anatoly Sharansky*: a computer scientist (Upon arrival in Israel, he changed his first name to Natan.);

Natalia Sharansky: his wife and supporter (Upon arrival in Israel, she changed her first name to Avital.)

When Anatoly Sharansky was a young man in Russia in the early 1970s, Jews could not freely attend synagogue, learn Hebrew, study Torah, or celebrate a Bar or Bat Mitzvah. In short, they could not practice Judaism in the way we take for granted. Neither could they leave the Soviet Union for freedom in Israel or the West. Yet ever since Golda Meir's stirring visit to Moscow (see Chapter 3), and more than ever after Israel's dra-

An anti-Semitic cartoon in a 1971 newspaper shows a "Zionist spider" crawling on a web whose strands say, "slander, lies, provocation, anti-Sovietism, Jewish question, and anti-communism."

Anatoly Sharansky, arrested in Russia in 1977 for his involvement in the movement to help Jews emigrate from Russia, took his first steps as a free man in 1986. With him were Ludwig Rehlinger (left), the German spy-swap negotiator, and Richard Burt (right), the American ambassador to Germany.

matic victory in the Six Day War of 1967, tens of thousands of Jews reawakened to their religion and to a desire to emigrate.

Anatoly Sharansky was one of these Jews. Sharansky became active in the movement to gain freedom not only for Jews but for all those suffering under the oppressive Communist regime. He worked closely with the physicist and dissident leader Andrei Sakharov, who was later honored with the Nobel Peace Prize. As a result of these activities, Sharansky was denied an exit visa in 1973, fired from his job, and harassed by the feared secret police, the KGB. In March 1977, at the age of 29, Sharansky was arrested on a Moscow street. For 16 months he was interrogated on the charge of treason, during which time the KGB compiled more than 50 volumes of "evidence" that he was an American spy.

Why do you think the Soviet Union was reluctant to let Jews emigrate from Russia?

Sharansky's trial and long imprisonment led to an international outcry that made him the best known Jewish dissident. Sentenced to a life term, Sharansky spent nine years in some of Russia's worst prisons, often in solitary confinement and freezing punishment cells. He went on several hunger strikes to protest the treatment he was receiving. He weighed 143 pounds when arrested; when freed, he was down to 77 pounds.

At the conclusion of his trial, Anatoly Sharansky spoke in stirring words of the Jewish longing for freedom. One of Sharansky's mottos during his confinement was, "They cannot humiliate me; only I can humiliate me."

Together and Yet Apart

Natalia and Anatoly Sharansky got married one day before Natalia used her exit visa and left for Jerusalem. For more than a decade, Natalia, who took the Hebrew name Avital when she reached Israel, devoted her life to winning her husband's freedom. She enlisted the support of the Jewish world and reached out to the leaders of the free world, including Presidents Jimmy Carter and Ronald Reagan. During a summit meeting in November 1985, President Reagan told President Mikhail Gorbachev (then head of the Soviet Union), "You can say again and again that Sharansky's a spy, but the world believes this lady, and you won't be able to change your image until you let him go."

The next year, Anatoly Sharansky was finally released. The world applauded as this small man strode across the border to freedom, taking only his prison clothes and a small Book of Psalms in Hebrew (given to him by his wife), which he had refused to abandon during all his years in prison.

Today Natan Sharansky lives in Jerusalem with his wife and their daughter. He continues to work on behalf of Jews in Russia and in Israel.

In 1996, he formed a new political party in Israel and became a government minister.

When Sharansky first arrived in Israel and was taken on dancing shoulders to the Western Wall, he said, "Holding our Psalm book in my hand, I kissed the wall and said, *Baruch matir asurim*. Blessed is the One who liberates the imprisoned."

Eyewitness to History

The first selection is from Sharansky's autobiography, *Fear No Evil*. In it, he recalls a seder he attended with Natalia shortly before he was arrested. The second selection is from the statement Sharansky made before the court that sentenced him to prison.

Avital and Natan Sharansky.

The special relevance of the Passover story to a group of refuseniks in Moscow was so obvious that nobody had to point it out. We sat there enthralled as we discussed the story of our ancestors, enslaved and oppressed in Egypt, a powerful land where they were unable to practice their religion or learn about their heritage. Then, through a series of miracles, they succeeded in leaving this place of bondage, eventually reaching their homeland, the land of Israel. That night I came across a moving line in the Passover liturgy that would stay with me forever: "In every generation, a person should feel as though he, personally, went out of Egypt." (It would be twelve long years before I could spend another Passover with Avital.)

Five years ago I submitted my application for exit to Israel. Now I'm further than ever from my dream. It would seem to be cause for regret. But it is absolutely otherwise. I am happy. I am happy that I lived honestly, in peace with my conscience. I never compromised my soul, even under the threat of death.

I am happy that I helped people. I am proud that I knew and worked with such honest, brave, and courageous people as Sakharov, Orlov, Ginzburg, who are carrying on the traditions of the Russian intelligentsia. I am fortunate to have been witness to the process of the liberation of Jews of the USSR.

I hope that the absurd accusation against me and the entire Jewish emigration movement will not hinder the liberation of my people. My near ones and friends know how I wanted to exchange activity in the emigration movement for a life with my wife, Avital, in Israel.

For more than 2,000 years the Jewish people, my people, have been dispersed. But wherever they are, wherever Jews are found, every year they have repeated, "Next year in Jerusalem." Now, when I am further than ever from my people, from Avital, facing many arduous years of imprisonment, I say, turning to my people, my Avital: Next year in Jerusalem.

Now I turn to you, the court, who were required to confirm a predetermined sentence: to you I have nothing to say.

How was it possible that Natan Sharansky managed to stay free on the "inside" even though he was forced to live in a prison?

Exploring the Mitzvah

Ḥerut

"All people, in every generation, must regard themselves as having been personally freed from Egypt." —PASSOVER HAGGADAH

The verse cited above may be the most emotionally moving in the entire Haggadah. Judaism insists that we never forget our origins. To cherish freedom, we must remember—spiritually and physically—that once we were slaves. The Torah itself repeatedly hearkens back to that experience with the refrain "For you were slaves in the land of Egypt."

Why do you think Judaism places such importance on remembering slavery? In what ways are you free that your ancestors were not?

LIVING THE MITZVAH

Help lead your Pesaḥ seder.

The seder is a celebration of our freedom. Find a special story about freedom and tell it at your seder.

There are many reasons why we are told to remember our liberation from slavery. First, we should never take our freedom for granted. To do so would be to lose our gratitude and appreciation, and our tradition knows that if we did that, we would become less vigilant about maintaining our own freedom.

Why does the Torah teach us to remember that we were slaves in the land of Egypt?

Second, when the Torah reminds us that we were strangers in Egypt, it reminds us to treat the stranger in our midst with dignity and justice. When the Bible describes Pharaoh's oppression of the Israelites, it creates empathy within us for the downtrodden of our own society today. Not just the Exodus, but the long history of the Jewish people instills us with a desire to "Proclaim liberty throughout all the land, unto all the inhabitants thereof." These words from Leviticus (25:10) are inscribed on the famous Liberty Bell in Philadelphia.

You may remember God's instruction to Moses to declare, "Let My people go!" But do you remember the second half of that verse? It is "Let My people go that they may serve Me." Judaism understands freedom as something more than the opportunity to do whatever you please. Freedom is not simply the absence of oppression, but the presence of meaningful choices in life, and the pursuit of them.

Avital Sharansky not only helped free her husband, but she was a leading figure in the fight to help all Russian refuseniks.

Can you spot the biblical quotation on the posters of the Jewish prisoners?

You could say that Natan Sharansky gained his freedom first by fighting the oppression of the Soviet Union and then, once he had moved to Israel, by continuing to work in behalf of all Soviet Jews.

In Our Ancestors' Footsteps

Another Jewish Trial: The Dreyfus Affair

When Anatoly Sharansky was brought before the Moscow court, many people began comparing the case to the Dreyfus affair, the most famous Jewish trial of the modern era.

Alfred Dreyfus (1859-1935) was a Jewish army officer in France. In the fall of 1894 he was accused of passing military secrets to the Germans. His trial divided all of France and aroused many anti-Semitic outbursts. Dreyfus was found guilty of treason and sentenced to the infamous Devil's Island prison off the coast of South America.

Alfred Dreyfus.

Dreyfus's family turned to supporters, who began uncovering all kinds of errors and inconsistencies in the trial. Not only was the evidence against Dreyfus speculative, but it was also found that the prosecution relied on forged documents. A real German spy, the probable culprit, was discovered. The verdict became a national scandal when the famed French novelist Emile Zola published an open letter to the president of France, entitled "J'accuse," in which he accused the army and the government of deliberately smearing Dreyfus's reputation.

Despite all the new evidence, Dreyfus was again found guilty in a second court-martial. Outrage at the verdict led to a major political shake-up of French government. In 1904 a new government ordered the court of appeals to reexamine the case. Two years later the court pronounced that the evidence against Dreyfus was unsubstantiated, and it declared him innocent of all charges.

One of the journalists following the Dreyfus case was Theodor Herzl. Herzl was so dismayed at what he saw—and at the anti-Semitism he had experienced in his native Vienna—that he began thinking that only a Jewish state could guarantee freedom from anti-Semitism. It was the Dreyfus affair that prompted the "father of Zionism" to begin his quest for a Jewish state.

Spotlight on the Bible: Moses and Judah Maccabee

When we think of champions of freedom, two great leaders of ancient Israel come to mind. The first, of course, is Moses. The slogan of the movement to free the Soviet Jews was the very words Moses spoke to Pharaoh: "Let My people go!" The old African-American spiritual of the same name also served as an anthem for the civil rights movement in America. Throughout history, Moses and the story of the Exodus have inspired many people in their search for freedom.

Judah Maccabee is another great champion of freedom. He led what some call the first revolt for religious freedom. Judah and his family refused to live under Syrian-Greek rule, which prohibited the practice of Judaism. Against over-whelming odds, but with plenty of conviction, the Maccabees rose up against their oppressors. Judah's father, Mattathias, is said to have sparked the rebellion when he replied to King Antiochus's officers:

> *Though all the nations within the king's dominions obey him . . . yet I and my sons and brothers will follow the covenant of our ancestors. Heaven forbid we should ever abandon the Law and its status. We will not obey the command of the king, nor will we deviate one step from our form of worship.* (I Maccabees 2:19-22)

As you remember, we celebrate each year at Passover the story of Moses and the liberation from Egyptian slavery, and at Ḥanukkah the victory that enabled Judah and his people to rededicate the Temple. *Can you think of other people from the Bible who risked their lives so that others could live freely as Jews?*

You Are There

Natan Sharansky wrote that his Soviet captors offered him a deal while in prison: if he would confess to the charges against him, he would be released from prison and allowed to emigrate to Israel.

Imagine that you are Natan Sharansky—alone, imprisoned, and in ill health. At times you despair of ever being set free and of seeing your wife and family again. At other times you know that you are suffering for a noble cause, and that your story is inspiring others to continue the struggle for freedom.

Make the arguments both for accepting and rejecting the deal with the authorities.

> ~ *Jewish Heroes Hall of Fame* ~
> Complete page 106 in the Jewish Heroes Hall of Fame.

7

TIKVAH תִּקְוָה

THE MITZVAH OF HOPE

"For we still love life . . . we still hope, hope about everthing."
—ANNE FRANK

Many ships during World War II brought refugees from Europe to safety in Palestine.

Tikvah is the mitzvah of hope. Through the darkest times of our history, Jews have clung to their hope and passed on their conviction that things will be better for the next generation. The Torah, recognizing that life often is difficult, commands us to "choose life." The prophets concurred, encouraging us all to "hope in Adonai."

The Diary

Time: Summer 1944

Place: Amsterdam, the Netherlands

Person: *Anne Frank*: a Jewish girl hiding with her family from the Nazis

On Anne Frank's thirteenth birthday, she received a book with a stiff cover and blank pages—a diary. In it, she wrote about all kinds of things: herself, her family, her friends, her teachers, schoolwork, and what she did for fun. Anne was a naturally cheerful person and a typical young teenager in many respects.

Anne Frank (second from left) at her tenth birthday party.

The house where Anne Frank lived.

But Anne Frank was living in Amsterdam in 1942, and she was Jewish. Holland had been invaded and was now occupied by the Nazis. Jews could not travel on the trolley. They could not go to the movies. They could not ride around the city on their bicycles. They could not even sit outside in the evening. In June 1942 the Jews were told they would have to leave their homes and their country.

The Nazis began deporting Dutch Jews, supposedly to "relocate" them in the East, but in reality the Nazis were transporting the Jews to their death in concentration camps.

Anne's father had prepared a few rooms in the back of his office building as a hiding place for the family. The entrance was blocked by a movable bookcase. Living in this space, Anne and her family had to be alert all the time. They could not be seen or heard. Friends of the family risked their own safety to supply Anne and her family with food and supplies.

What did Anne do, day after day, week after week, month after month, in the silence and emptiness of the cramped living space? She read, and read, and wrote in her diary. She looked out the window, and dreamed, and hoped.

Hope Discovered

After two years, on August 4, 1944, someone betrayed the Frank family, and the German police discovered their hiding place. Anne was sent to the Westerbork concentration camp, was moved to Auschwitz-Birkenau, and then taken to Bergen-Belsen. There she died in March 1945, two months before Holland was freed, and three months before her sixteenth birthday.

Anne's diary was discovered in the Franks' hiding place after the war. Although it was initially rejected by publishers, *The Diary of Anne Frank* went on to become famous all over the world. Anne Frank's story reached even more people when it was adapted as a dramatic play and then as a movie. The building where Anne hid has become a museum, and a foundation established in her name promotes the study of peace, especially among youth.

The following section contains excerpts from Anne Frank's diary that testify to her indomitable spirit and undying hope.

Eyewitness to History

These are Anne Frank's own words, excerpted from her diary.

Friday, December 24, 1943

Believe me, if you have been shut up for a year and a half, it can get too much for you some days . . . you can't crush your feelings. Cycling, dancing, whistling, looking out into the world, feeling young, to know that I'm free—that's what I long for; still I mustn't show it, because I sometimes think if all eight of us began to pity ourselves, or went about with discontented faces, where would it lead us?

Tuesday, March 7, 1944

And in the evening, when I lie in bed and end my prayers with the words, "I thank you, God, for all that is good and dear and beautiful," I am filled with joy. . . . I've found that there is always some beauty left—in nature, sunshine, freedom, in yourself; these can all help you. Look at these things, then you find yourself again, and God, and then you regain your balance.

And whoever is happy will make others happy too. He who has courage and faith will never perish in misery.

Friday, April 14, 1944

My work, my hope, my love, my courage, all these things keep my head above water and keep me from complaining.

Wednesday, May 3, 1944

I am young and strong and am living a great adventure . . . I have been given a lot, a happy nature, a great deal of cheerfulness and strength. Every day I feel that I am developing inwardly, that the liberation is drawing nearer and how beautiful nature is, how good the people are about me, how interesting this adventure is. Why, then, should I be in despair?

Friday, May 26, 1944

We still hope, hope against everything.

Saturday, July 15, 1944

It's really a wonder that I haven't dropped all my ideals, because they seem so absurd and impossible to carry out. Yet I keep them, because in spite of everything I still believe that people are really good at heart. I simply can't build up my hopes on a foundation consisting of confusion, misery, and death. I see the world gradually being turned into a wilderness, I hear the ever approaching thunder, which will destroy us too, I can feel the sufferings of millions and yet, if I look up into the heavens, I think that it will all come right, that this cruelty too will end, and that peace and tranquility will return again.

In the meantime, I must uphold my ideals, for perhaps the time will come when I shall be able to carry them out.

Anne Frank.

How was Anne Frank able to hold on to hope?

Exploring the Mitzvah

Tikvah

"As long as there is life, there is hope."

—Jerusalem Talmud, Berachot 9:1

The ideal of hope runs deep in the Jewish soul. As the words of Israel's national anthem, "Hatikvah," point out, Jews have kept hope alive through 2,000 years of wandering and tragedy. We are here today as Jews because our ancestors never gave up hope.

The German edition of Anne Frank's diary featured a letter written in her own handwriting.

The subject of hope often appears in the writing of Elie Wiesel. Wiesel is a survivor of the Holocaust and a world-famous author. In 1986 he was awarded the Nobel Peace Prize. In an essay entitled "Against Despair," Wiesel described a scene he witnessed in the concentration camps. Even

Bring a smile to the face of someone who needs one.

Cheer up someone you know by doing something special for him or her. Your class can cheer up someone you don't know by visiting a local nursing home before a Jewish holiday and bringing a small gift with you.

in that place of death, the Jews celebrated the festival of Simhat Torah. They had no synagogue and no Torah scrolls. But when someone picked up a young boy and started dancing around as if he were a Torah scroll, the others joined in, dancing, singing, and crying. "Never before had Jews celebrated Simhat Torah with such fervor."

Wiesel retells a story about the Hasidic Rabbi Nahman of Bratslav that illustrates our unwillingness to lose hope:

> One day Hasidim came to inform the great Rebbe Nahman of Bratzlav of renewed persecutions of Jews in the Ukraine. The Master listened and said nothing. Then they told him of pogroms in certain villages. Again the Master listened and said nothing. Then they told of slaughtered families, of desecrated cemeteries, of children burned alive. The Master listened and shook his head. "I know," he whispered, "I know what you want. I know. You want me to shout with pain, weep in despair, I know, I know. But I will not, you hear me, I will not." Then after a long silence, he did begin to shout, louder and louder, "Gevalt, Yiden, zeit nit meyaesh! *Jews, do not despair!*"

The eighteenth-century French philosopher Voltaire wrote, "When all hope is gone, death becomes a duty." Elie Wiesel disagreed. "Not so for Jews. When all hope is gone, Jews invent new hopes. Even in the midst of despair, we attempt to justify hope."

In Our Ancestors' Footsteps

Israel's National Anthem

Why are Jews so dedicated to keeping hope alive?

Israel's national anthem is called "Hatikvah," which means "The Hope." The words to the anthem are taken (with a few changes) from a poem written in 1878 by Naphtali Herz Imber. Imber died in 1909, well before the state of Israel was established.

The words of "Hatikvah" in Hebrew and English appear below. See if you can find the two Hebrew forms of the word *tikvah* in the poem. Then read the translation, and complete these two sentences:

1. The hope expressed in this poem is . . .
2. My hope for the Jewish people is . . .

Within the heart	כָּל עוֹד בַּלֵּבָב פְּנִימָה
a Jewish spirit is still alive	נֶפֶשׁ יְהוּדִי הוֹמִיָּה
and the eyes look eastward	וּלְפַאֲתֵי מִזְרָח קָדִימָה
toward Zion.	עַיִן לְצִיּוֹן צוֹפִיָּה
Our hope is not lost,	עוֹד לֹא אָבְדָה תִּקְוָתֵנוּ
the hope of two thousand years	הַתִּקְוָה בַּת שְׁנוֹת אַלְפַּיִם
to be a free nation in our land	לִהְיוֹת עַם חָפְשִׁי בְּאַרְצֵנוּ
in the land of Zion and Jerusalem.	אֶרֶץ צִיּוֹן וִירוּשָׁלַיִם

SPOTLIGHT ON THE BIBLE: JEREMIAH

One of the earliest tragedies faced by our ancestors was the destruction of the kingdom of Judah by the Babylonians more than 2,500 years ago. In 586 B.C.E., King Nebuchadnezzar destroyed the Temple in Jerusalem, demolished much of the city and the country, and sent many of the leaders of Judah into exile. It was a time of grief and despair for the Jewish people.

The prophet Jeremiah lived through these events. Like the other prophets of Israel, Jeremiah criticized his fellow Jews for their moral weakness and their role in bringing upon themselves such misfortune. Yet Jeremiah and the prophets also proclaimed a strong message of consolation and hope. They insisted that the people should not feel abandoned and that their destroyed country would be restored. Jeremiah went so far as to purchase land in his hometown of Anathoth in the middle of the war. He told everybody that he was confident that life would return to normal in the not too distant future.

Here are some words of comfort and hope from Jeremiah 32 and 33, which the prophet spoke in God's name:

Houses, fields, and vineyards shall again be purchased in this land.

I will bring them back to this place and let them dwell secure. They shall be My people, and I shall be their God.

I will make an everlasting covenant with them . . . and I will plant them in this land faithfully, with all My heart and soul.

Again there shall be heard in this place, which you say is ruined . . . in the cities of Judah and the streets of Jerusalem . . . the sound of mirth and gladness, the voice of the groom and the voice of the bride. . . ."

(Jeremiah 32,33)

You Are There

Imagine that you were a pen pal with Anne Frank before the war and that even after Anne went into hiding, you two were able to smuggle letters back and forth. In her private letters to you, Anne becomes increasingly depressed about her situation. You consider Anne a friend, although you have never met, and are concerned about her feelings.

After you receive her latest letter, in which she fears she can no longer bear living in hiding and wonders whether the Nazis are going to discover her any day, you sit down and write her a letter to make her feel hope again. *What would you write?*

┌───┐
│   │
│   ~ **Jewish Heroes Hall of Fame** ~   │
│   Complete page 107 in the Jewish Heroes Hall of Fame. │
│   │
└───┘

8

TZEDEK   צֶדֶק

THE MITZVAH OF JUSTICE

"Let justice well up as waters, and righteousness as a mighty stream."
—AMOS 5:24

Tzedek is the mitzvah of doing justice. A major concern of Judaism is the creation of a just society. The Torah and indeed all Jewish law (halachah) repeatedly stress the need for a system of justice that is impartial, equally serving the rich and the poor, the powerful and the powerless. Pictured above is the statue of "Justice" in front of the Supreme Court, Washington D.C.

A Passion for Justice

Setting the Scene ✸ ✸ ✸ ✸ ✸

Time: June 15, 1993

Place: Washington, D.C.

Person: *Ruth Bader Ginsburg*: lawyer, professor, and judge

When Ruth Bader Ginsburg was a law student at Harvard University in 1960, the dean of her school recommended her for the prestigious job of law clerk to a famous Supreme Court justice. The justice responded to the dean that while the candidate was impressive, he just wasn't ready to hire a woman. When Ruth Bader Ginsburg graduated with honors from Columbia Law School, not one law firm in New York was willing to hire her. Again, the companies were not prepared to hire a woman lawyer.

Ruth Ginsburg, rejected by the male establishment, became a pioneer in the fight for women's legal rights. As director of the Women's Rights Project of the American Civil Liberties Union, she argued before the Supreme Court six landmark cases on behalf of women. She won five of

Ruth Bader Ginsburg accompanying President Bill Clinton en route to the press conference where Clinton announced her nomination to the Supreme Court.

the six cases. Inspired by the civil rights progress made by blacks, Ginsburg helped convince the Supreme Court that discrimination in the law between men and women was based on unfair and harmful stereotypes and denied women the constitutional right to equal representation.

Where None Had Gone Before

Ginsburg became the first female law professor on the faculty of Columbia University. In 1980, President Jimmy Carter appointed her to the United States Court of Appeals for the District of Columbia, the second highest court in the country. She served there with distinction for thirteen years. In 1993, President Bill Clinton nominated her to the Supreme Court.

At her nomination hearings, Ginsburg was called "the Thurgood Marshall of gender equality law," after the great black Supreme Court justice who helped end segregation and pioneer racial equality. Ginsburg became only the second woman and the sixth Jew to sit on the Supreme Court.

In her acceptance speech at the White House, Ginsburg paid special tribute to her mother, who died when Ruth was 17 years old. Her words brought tears to the eyes of the president, and to many of those gathered at the historic occasion.

What were some of Justice Ginsburg's early encounters with discrimination that led her to fight for equal rights for women?

Eyewitness to History

The passages below are from Ruth Bader Ginsburg's own words, upon her accepting the nomination to the Supreme Court, and from her Senate confirmation hearings.

On Her Background

Neither of my parents had the means to attend college, but both taught me to love learning, to care about people, and to work hard for whatever I wanted or believed in.

Their parents had the foresight to leave the old country when Jewish ancestry and faith meant exposure to pogroms and denigration of one's human worth.

I am very sensitized to discrimination. I grew up at the time of World War II in a Jewish family. I have memories as a child, even before the war, of being in a car with my parents and driving places . . . and there

Ruth Bader Ginsburg.

was a sign in front of a restaurant, and it said, "No dogs or Jews allowed." That existed in this country during my childhood.

And then one couldn't help but be sensitive to discrimination, living as a Jew in America at the time of World War II.

On Justice for All

I think rank discrimination against anyone is against the tradition of the United States and is to be deplored. Rank discrimination is not part of our nation's culture. Tolerance is. This country is great because of its accommodation of diversity. The richness of the diversity of this country is a treasure, and it's a constant challenge, too, to remain tolerant and respectful of one another.

"We the people" was not then [the days of the founding fathers] what it is today . . . [The Constitution] had certain limitations, blind spots . . . [but] the beauty of this Constitution is that through a combination of interpretation, constitutional amendment, laws passed by Congress, "we the people" has grown ever larger. So now it includes people who were once in bondage, it includes women, who were left out of the political community at the start.

On Justice

Laws as protectors of the oppressed, the poor, the loner, is evident in the work of my Jewish predecessors on the Supreme Court. The Biblical command: "justice, justice shalt thou pursue" is a strand that ties them together. I keep those words on the wall of my chambers, as an ever-present reminder of what judges must do "that they may thrive."

On Justice for Women

I remain an advocate of the equal rights amendment, I will tell you, for this reason: because I have a daughter and a granddaughter, and I would like the legislature of this country to stand up and say, "We want to make a clarion call that women and men are equal before the law."

I have a last thank-you. It is to my mother, Celia Amster Bader, the bravest and strongest person I have known, who was taken from me much too soon. I pray that I may be all that she would have been had she lived in an age when women could aspire and achieve, and daughters are cherished as much as sons.

Exploring the Mitzvah

Tzedek

"Justice, justice shall you pursue." —Deuteronomy 16:20

Lawyer Sam Leibowitz, center, won the acquittal of black youths falsely charged with the rape of two white women in the famed Scottsboro case.

The words *tzedek* and *tzedakah* appear almost 300 times in the Torah! Our tradition teaches that justice is one of the two most important qualities that sustain society. (The other is compassion.) In the heart of the

Torah, the Holiness Code (Leviticus 19) links being holy with being just. There we are commanded:

You shall not steal.

You shall not deal deceitfully.

You shall not defraud.

You shall not commit robbery.

You shall pay a laborer on time.

You shall not insult the deaf.

You shall not place a stumbling block before the blind.

You shall not render an unfair decision.

You shall not favor the rich or the poor.

You shall judge your fellow fairly.

You shall not take vengeance or bear a grudge.

You shall love your neighbor as yourself.

Which of the commandments listed here do you think are most important to help us lead just lives?

Since biblical times, Judaism deemed a fair and efficient court system to be essential to the creation of a just society. One of the Torah portions in Deuteronomy begins with the commandment to "appoint judges and clerks for your tribes, in all your settlements." When the Israelites had their own nation, the Sanhedrin functioned as the supreme court. In the diaspora, every Jewish community had a *beit din*, or local court. Jewish law (halachah) contains many rules about how cases are to be tried and who can be a witness.

In this midrash (Leviticus Rabbah 25:1), the rabbis state:

Explain in your own words the meaning of this midrash.

If a great scholar, known for observing all the commandments, is able to protest against injustice but does not, that person is cursed.

If a simple person, who is not known for observing all the commandments, protests against injustice, that person is blessed.

Tzedek, like the other commandments, is a universal responsibility. Even if we are unsure of what will be accomplished, we are not free to desist from seeking justice. Elie Wiesel once told this story:

What does the man in this story mean when he says, "If I continue my protest, at least I will prevent others from changing me"?

A man saw the injustice of his city, and decided to protest. Every day he protested. People made fun of him, and derided him. One day a passerby stopped and asked the man: "Why do you continue to protest? Can't you see no one is paying attention? Can't you see that nothing will change?"

The man answered: "I will tell you why I continue. In the beginning, I thought I would change people. Today, I know I will not. Yet, if I continue my protest, at least I will prevent others from changing me."

In Our Ancestors' Footsteps

Jews and the Supreme Court

Many great American Jews have served the United States as lawyers and judges.

Louis Brandeis.

Louis Brandeis was the first Jewish Supreme Court justice, serving from 1916 to 1939. His "Brandeis brief," in which he persuaded the Supreme Court that minimum-hours legislation for women was reasonable, revolutionized the practice of law. An advocate of social and economic reforms, he was nicknamed "The People's Attorney." Brandeis was also a leading Zionist figure. Brandeis University, one of America's best schools, is named after him.

Benjamin Cardozo served on the Supreme Court from 1932 until his death in 1938. He too was highly influential in relating the law to social change. The school of law at Yeshiva University is named after him.

Felix Frankfurter, a close associate of Brandeis, succeeded him and served more than twenty years, from 1939 to 1962. Before he joined the court, he helped create the American Civil Liberties Union.

Three other Jews have been named to the Supreme Court: Arthur Goldberg and Abe Fortas both served in the 1960s; Stephen Breyer was named to the Court in 1994.

Spotlight on the Bible: Abraham

Abraham is often spoken of as the father of the Jewish people. The Torah recalls that it was Abraham who first heard the call to journey to Canaan and establish a new people with a new faith. An incident in Abraham's life reflects how this faith was indelibly tied to the doing of justice.

According to the Torah (Genesis 18), God revealed to Abraham that the cities of Sodom and Gomorrah would be destroyed because their inhabitants were exceedingly wicked. Abraham was troubled by this revelation. He was upset that God would think of destroying an entire city, where there must have been both innocent and guilty people. Abraham decided to question God— even more, to demand justice from God! Below is a paraphrase of the conversation between Abraham and God:

> *Abraham: Will You sweep away the innocent with the guilty? Shall not the Judge of all the earth deal justly? If there are fifty innocent people, will You save the city?*
>
> *God:　Yes.*
>
> *Abraham: If there are forty-five innocent people, will You save the city?*
>
> *God:　Yes.*
>
> *Abraham: If there are forty innocent people, will You save the city?*
>
> *God:　Yes.*
>
> *Abraham: If there are thirty innocent people, will You save the city?*
>
> *God:　Yes.*
>
> *Abraham: If there are twenty innocent people, will You save the city?*
>
> *God:　Yes.*
>
> *Abraham: If there are ten innocent people, will You save the city?*
>
> *God:　Yes.*

How do Abraham's negotiations with God reflect both Abraham's and God's beliefs in justice?

Only when Abraham realized there weren't even ten righteous people did he stop bargaining with God.

You Are There

One of the cases Ruth Ginsburg faced as a federal appeals judge was *Goldman v. Weinberger* (1984). Goldman was a Jewish captain who petitioned the U.S. Air Force to allow him to wear a *kippah* while on duty. He argued that the practice was essential to his religious expression as an Orthodox Jew, and he pointed out that he had already worn it in the military without incident for several years.

The air force countered that the military required obedience to regulations, including dress codes, which specify exactly what a soldier can wear while on duty.

Imagine that you are Judge Ginsburg deciding this case. How would you vote, and why?

After discussing this issue, you may find out about this case by reading below.

The D.C. Circuit Court of Appeals let stand the air force regulation banning the wearing of a *kippah* while on duty. However, Judge Ginsburg dissented from that ruling, commenting that the majority opinion reflected "callous indifference" to Goldman's religious faith and was counter to "the best of our tradition." The Supreme Court narrowly (5-4) upheld the decision, but Congress later enacted legislation that effectively overturned it, and so today Jews are permitted to wear *kippot* in the U.S. military.

LIVING THE MITZVAH

Learn the alphabet of justice.

Do you know what A.D.L. stands for? What about A.C.L.U? Ever heard of the S.P.L.C.? All three are very important organizations to know about. Perhaps you could do a report about one of these justice organizations.

> ## ~ *Jewish Heroes Hall of Fame* ~
> Complete page 108 in the Jewish Heroes Hall of Fame.

9 PIKUAḤ NEFESH פִּקּוּחַ נֶפֶשׁ

THE MITZVAH OF SAVING A LIFE

"Saving one life is like saving an entire world."
—AVOT OF RABBI NATAN

By the 1980s, a combination of civil war and drought had brought Ethiopia's Jews to the brink of starvation. In 1985, the Israeli government boarded 8,000 Ethiopian Jews onto air force planes during a secret airlift that brought them safely to Israel. The emergency rescue mission was called Operation Moses.

Pikuah Nefesh is the mitzvah of saving a life. Judaism teaches that a human life is holy. To save a life is thus a responsibility that supersedes virtually every other commandment.

THE ENTEBBE RESCUE

Time: July 3, 1976

Place: Entebbe, Uganda

People: *Yonatan Netanyahu*: commander of an Israeli commando unit;
250 passengers on board a hijacked Air France flight

On July 3, 1976, just as America was about to celebrate its 200th birthday, Israel launched one of the most daring military rescue missions in history.

An Air France flight had left Tel Aviv, stopped over in Athens, and was en route to Paris when a band of trained hijackers took control. They diverted the plane and its more than 250 passengers to Uganda, where

The Entebbe hostages celebrate their liberation at Ben-Gurion Airport in Tel Aviv.

the notorious dictator Idi Amin was apparently in collusion with the terrorists.

The terrorists released half the hostages; but they separated out and kept captive all passengers with Israeli passports or Jewish names. The terrorists threatened to execute the hostages unless dozens of terrorists were released—most of them held in Israeli prisons. While the Israeli government negotiated to extend the deadline, it also made secret preparations to attempt a rescue.

The rescue mission seemed foolhardy. First, scores of Israeli commandos and equipment needed to be flown undetected over thousands of miles of unfriendly airspace. These commandos would have to overcome the Ugandan security forces, then find and storm the airport building where the hostages were being kept. They would have to eliminate the heavily armed terrorists in a matter of seconds to prevent the slaughter of the hostages.

Why do you think the Israeli government chose to attempt a military rescue at Entebbe, rather than negotiate a settlement?

The Israelis put to use every bit of their intelligence-gathering capability to build a mock-up of the Entebbe airport at a military base in Israel, and they practiced the strike over and over again.

Birth of a Hero

Leading the raid was Yonatan Netanyahu. The son of a prominent Jewish historian, "Yoni" had grown up in both Israel and the United States. As a combat officer, he was wounded in battle during the Six-Day War of 1967, and was left with a partial disability in one hand. After the Yom Kippur War of 1973, Yoni was awarded Israel's highest military decoration for bravery in combat. He went on to study philosophy at Harvard University. He later returned to Israel and despite his disability, was named to head an elite commando unit.

The Entebbe rescue has entered the annals of military legend. The commando force was on the ground barely 90 minutes. It caught the Ugandans and the terrorists completely by surprise. The hostages were freed with but a handful of casualties. Close to 100 innocent lives were saved. Only one soldier was fatally wounded in the operation: Yonatan Netanyahu.

Yoni was shot while directing his men during the assault, and he died as his plane was returning to Israel.

Eyewitness to History

Yonatan Netanyahu was not only a soldier but also a philosopher and a wonderful letter writer. The first excerpt below is from a letter he wrote when he was 17 years old. The second is from one he wrote five days before the raid on Entebbe.

Yoni Netanyahu.

Death . . . does not frighten me. It arouses my curiosity. It is an enigma that I, like many others, have tried to fathom without success. I do not fear it because I attribute little value to a life without purpose. And if it is necessary for me to lay down my life in the attainment of the goal I'll set for it, I will do so willingly. . . .

I remember a few years ago there was a whole month of nothing but field operations and on three consecutive occasions I had encounters with Arabs, and on one of them I killed a man, for the first time at such close range. . . . It adds a whole dimension of sadness to a man's being. Not a momentary, passing sadness, but something that sort of sinks in and is forgotten, yet is there and endures. . . .

In the army I have learned to appreciate the beauty of life, the immense pleasure of sleep, the taste of water which is irreplaceable, the matchless value of will power and all the wonderful things a man can do if he only wants to. . . . I have always said that my time in Zahal [the Israel

What did Yonatan Netanyahu learn from his army training?

Defense Force] is something that I have to live through and make the best of it. Now, even though it is a stretch of road which I shall not follow for the rest of my life, it has become deeply meaningful for me. I know that without this period I would be lacking something. I would probably not be aware I was missing it but for being in the army, and my life would probably go on quite normally and be as complete as before. But since I am here, I find to my great joy and surprise a life that *has no equal.* . . .

When you see death face to face, when you know there is every chance that you too may die, when you are wounded, and alone, in the midst of a scorched field, surrounded by smoke-mushrooms from exploding shells with your arm shattered and burning with a terrible pain, when you're bleeding and want water more than anything else—then life becomes more precious and craved-for than ever. You want to embrace it and go on with it, to escape from all the blood and death, to live. . . .

I am doing things because they have to be done and not because I want to. And the same haunting question comes up—can I let myself live like this, work like this, and wear myself out? The answer is always that I must go on and finish what I have begun—that I have an obligation not only to the job, but to myself as well. . . .

Exploring the Mitzvah

Pikuaḥ Nefesh

"Do not stand idly by the blood of your fellow."

—LEVITICUS 19:16

LIVING THE MITZVAH

Volunteer to help at a blood drive.

Find out if your synagogue or community center is organizing one. If not, contact the American Red Cross in your vicinity.

Again and again the Torah commands us to be responsible for each other's lives: "You shall love your neighbor as yourself."

Why is saving a life so important? The answer appears at the very beginning of the Torah, where we are told that God created man and woman in God's image. This means that every person in some way bears the image of God. When we save a life, we save something that is infinitely precious and holy.

The rabbis have noted that when Cain slew Abel, only a few people existed on earth. The loss of Abel nearly meant the extinction of the whole human race. They derived a moral from the story: To save a life is tantamount to saving all of humanity.

From the quotation at the beginning of this section, our sages concluded that each of us has a responsibility to act when confronted with a situation in which a life can be saved. If you are in a situation in which someone can be rescued, or a threat to a human life can be eliminated, you are commanded to act even if risks are involved.

Henrietta Szold (1860-1945), founder of Hadassah, the women's Zionist organization, devoted much of her energy to the mitzvah of Pikuaḥ Nefesh. She became director of Youth Aliyah, which saved the lives of thousands of Jewish children from the Nazis, and she helped establish Hadassah Hospital in Israel.

LIVING THE MITZVAH

Donate money to an organization that saves lives.

Among the many worthy groups that help in emergency situations around the world are the Joint Distribution Committee (a Jewish organization) and the International Rescue Committee (founded by Albert Einstein).

Saving a life is more important than virtually all other mitzvot. A sick and weak person is encouraged to eat on Yom Kippur—because of Pikuaḥ Nefesh. For security reasons, soldiers and other personnel remain on duty during Shabbat or Rosh Hashanah—because of Pikuaḥ Nefesh.

A special category of Pikuaḥ Nefesh, which applies to the Entebbe rescue, is called Pidyon Sh'vuyim (freeing of captives). This is the responsibility to save fellow Jews who are being held captive. Historically, this usually meant the paying of ransom money to those holding the captives. Jewish law insists that even moneys set aside for charitable or synagogue purposes should be used to free imprisoned Jews. Maimonides stated that a person who delays the fulfillment of this duty and prolongs a fellow Jew's imprisonment should be regarded as a criminal.

More recently, Pidyon Sh'vuyim has come to mean the utilizing of all means at one's disposal, from economic (money) to political (lobbying), in order to free Jews who are held captive. During the 1970s and 1980s, the American Jewish community worked hard to convince the Soviet Union to let its Jews emigrate. Jews saw this as fulfilling the mitzvah of Pidyon Sh'vuyim.

In Our Ancestors' Footsteps

Dona Gracia Nasi

Dona Gracia Nasi (1510-1569) is one of the great figures of Jewish history. She was a Portuguese Marrano, a person who converted to Christianity in order to escape persecution by the Spanish Inquisition, but inwardly remained Jewish. The Inquisition was zealously seeking out Jews who claimed to be Catholic, and torturing them and putting them to death. After her husband's death, she took over his successful banking establishment.

Can you recall an incident you read about in the newspaper where the mitzvah of Pikuaḥ Nefesh was fulfilled?

Dona Gracia was forced to move repeatedly during her life to escape the Inquisition. She fled from Portugal to Flanders to Venice and then to Ferrara in Italy, and finally to Constantinople in Turkey, where she openly returned to Judaism. Despite her own difficult circumstances, Dona Gracia devoted her fortune to helping the Jewish people.

Dona Gracia established schools and synagogues in Constantinople. She was also a Zionist long before the term officially came into being. Dona Gracia succeeded in getting permission from the Turkish sultan to begin rebuilding the ancient city of Tiberias on the shores of the Sea of Galilee in Palestine.

Foremost among Dona Gracia's activities was the mitzvah of Pikuaḥ Nefesh. For years she worked to organize the flight of fugitive Marranos, like herself, from Portugal. Dona Gracia's efforts saved thousands of lives.

Gracia Nasi, portrayed on a 1553 medal.

Spotlight on the Bible: Yocheved and Pharaoh's Daughter

The life of Moses, one of the most important people in Jewish history, was almost over before it began. When Moses was born, the Egyptian pharaoh had decreed that all male Jewish children were to be put to death. Yocheved, Moses's mother, hid him for three months, but then she knew she could not continue to keep him hidden. Yocheved put Moses in a basket by the banks of the river and had his sister, Miriam, watch to see what happened.

> *Now the daughter of Pharaoh came down to bathe at the river, and her maidens walked beside the river; she saw the basket among the reeds and sent her maid to fetch it. When she opened it, she saw the child; and, the baby was crying. She took pity on him and said, "This is one of the Hebrews' children." Then his sister said to Pharaoh's daughter "Shall I go and call you a nurse from the Hebrew women to nurse the child for you?" And Pharaoh's daughter said to her, "Go." So the girl went and called the child's mother. And Pharaoh's daughter said to her, "Take this child away and nurse him for me, and I will give you your wages." So the woman took the child and nursed him. And the child grew and she brought him to Pharaoh's daughter, and he became her son. (Exodus 2:5-10)*

Pharaoh's daughter knew she had saved a life. But she had no idea that Moses would become the Jewish people's greatest prophet, leader, and teacher.

You Are There

Imagine you are the commander of an Israeli commando unit. Some Israelis have been kidnapped and terrorists are threatening to murder them.

Your superior officer details his plan for freeing the captives. He informs you that even if the plan works, there's a 50-50 chance of your dying in the raid. You have the right to refuse to go. Do you decline, or do you lead the raid?

If you decline, how good would the odds need to be in order for you to accept?

⮞ Jewish Heroes Hall of Fame ⮜

Complete pages 109 and 110 in the Jewish Heroes Hall of Fame.

10 TZEDAKAH צְדָקָה

THE MITZVAH OF CHARITY

"You shall not harden your heart, nor shut your hand from your brother in need. . . ."
—DEUTERONOMY 15:7

Tzedakah is the mitzvah of helping the poor. It is often translated as "charity." However, charity is usually understood as a voluntary act. Tzedakah, according to our tradition, is a responsibility from which no one is exempt. Tzedakah is sometimes called "economic justice," because it is from the same Hebrew root as *tzedek*, which refers to "political justice." Tzedakah implies sharing your wealth with those in need. The girls in this photo are dressed as giant tzedakah boxes to remind us to be generous when we give Tzedakah.

FOR THE SAKE OF MY BROTHERS

Time: The early 1920s through 1954
Place: New York and other major cities
People: *Albert Einstein*: one of the greatest scientists of all time;
Chaim Weizmann: a great scientist, Zionist, and Israel's first president

Albert Einstein once began a speech by admitting, "It is no easy matter for me to overcome my natural inclination to a life of quiet contemplation."

Yet that is precisely what Albert Einstein did. Many of the people well acquainted with Einstein's scientific accomplishments may be unaware of his dedication to social justice in general, and his commitment to Tzedakah in particular. The man who created the theory of relativity, who wrote three theses by the age of 23, each of which changed the world of physics forever, devoted much of his time to charitable acts. He was involved in movements to improve education, in several world peace movements, and the raising of money for many deserving charities.

When Albert Einstein first visited the United States in 1921, the Nobel Prize winner was given a hero's ticker-tape welcome parade in New York.

A tzedakah box from Eastern Europe with the Ten Commandments on it.

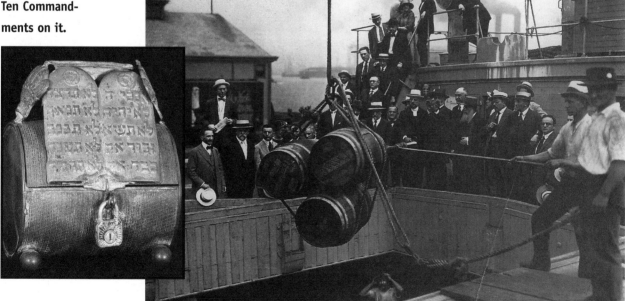

Tzedakah does not always take the form of money. The Jewish tradition of caring for others, part of the mitzvah of Tzedakah, can be expressed in many ways. The photo above, taken at New York Harbor in 1919, shows rabbis assisting with the first shipment of kosher meat that was sent to the starving Jews of Poland.

Yet Einstein spent much of his time during this trip doing acts of Tzedakah! Einstein was traveling at the behest of Chaim Weizmann, a renowned Zionist leader (and fellow scientist), who would become the first president of the State of Israel. Einstein and Weizmann traveled around the country explaining the Zionist idea of creating a new Jewish state, and raising sorely needed funds to help settlers in Palestine. Einstein played an especially important role in convincing Jewish doctors to support the establishment of a medical school at the Hebrew University of Jerusalem.

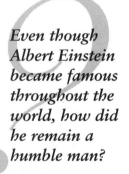

Although Albert Einstein claimed he wasn't religious, in what ways did he exhibit religious values?

Indeed, Albert Einstein was so helpful that upon the death of his friend Chaim Weizmann, he was asked to become the second president of Israel. Einstein's reply to Abba Eban, the Israeli ambassador in Washington, D.C., stated, "I am deeply moved by the offer . . . [but] unsuited to fulfill the duties of that high office. . . . I am the more distressed over these circumstances because my relationship to the Jewish people has become my strongest human bond."

Helping in a Time of Need

As the clouds of fascism and war darkened over Europe in the 1930s, Albert Einstein broadened his help to all refugees in need, regardless of race or religion. In 1933, he helped found the International Rescue Committee, which is today one of the most important refugee assistance organizations in the world. In 1935, he joined with Alfred E. Smith, a former governor of New York, to raise funds for the American Christian Committee for German Refugees and the Emergency Committee in Aid of Political Refugees. Einstein would often play his violin at charity concerts and pose for portraits.

Even though Albert Einstein became famous throughout the world, how did he remain a humble man?

Einstein refused to benefit personally from the large sums that were offered to him for speaking engagements and writing. When refugees sought him at his home in Princeton, New Jersey, he went out of his way to help them directly, giving them clothes and money and writing letters of recommendation to help them secure jobs. The man who personified the highest ideal of genius also embodied the highest ideal of Tzedakah.

Eyewitness to History

Below are Albert Einstein's own words, as excerpted from his writings and speeches.

The pursuit of knowledge for its own sake, an almost fanatical love of justice, and the desire for personal independence—these are the features of the Jewish tradition which make me thank my stars that I belong to it.

Today every Jew feels that to be a Jew means to bear a serious responsibility not only to his own community, but to humanity.

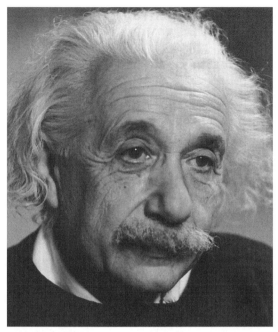
Albert Einstein.

The life of the individual has meaning only insofar as it aids in making the life of every living thing nobler and more beautiful.

The bond that has united the Jews for thousands of years and that unites them today is, above all, the democratic ideal of social justice, coupled with the ideal of mutual aid and tolerance among all men. Even the most ancient religious scriptures of the Jews are steeped in these social ideas, which have powerfully affected Christianity and Mohammed-anism and have had a benign influence upon the social structure of a great part of mankind. The introduction of a weekly day of rest should be remembered here—a profound blessing to all mankind. Personalities such as Moses, Spinoza, and Karl Marx, dissimilar as they may be, all lived and sacrificed themselves for the ideal of social justice; and it was the tradition of their forefathers that led them on this thorny path. The unique accomplishments of the Jews in the field of philanthropy spring from the same source.

Exploring the Mitzvah

Tzedakah

"Whoever sees a person in need requesting help,
and ignores that person,
and refuses to give tzedakah,
transgresses the commandment:
Do not harden your heart,
and do not withhold your hand,
from your brother in need."

(Maimonides, Laws of Tzedakah 7:2)

The Torah tells us we must give to the less fortunate. But it also reminds us that we must care about the dignity of poor people. In biblical times, a needy person did not have to go to a farmer and beg for grain or even for permission to glean (to collect the grain that the harvesters over-looked or dropped). Instead, the Torah tells the farmer to leave the cor-ners of the field unpicked entirely—that section belonged to the poor, and they were entitled to the grain and crops from that area. Also, the farmer could not call his poor sister or cousin to come to collect the grain. All

Create a family tzedakah box.

Place the box in a central location in your home and encourage your family to deposit change in the box every day. Decide with your family where the tzedakah money should go.

poor people could come and take what they wanted. This special kind of Tzedakah also applied to a farmer's vineyards and orchards.

We may not be farmers today, but the principle of setting aside a portion of our "field" (our income) remains a responsibility and a challenge. The Jewish community in America practices the mitzvah of Tzedakah through many charitable organizations. The single largest one is called the United Jewish Appeal. Every year the UJA organizes scores of fund-raising events, including "Super Sunday," when a massive telephone campaign attempts to get all involved members of the Jewish community to make an annual Tzedakah pledge. The millions of dollars raised by the UJA are divided among local Jewish organizations (such as Jewish community centers, family services, nursing homes, and day schools), as well as those in Israel.

Tzedakah has come to mean sharing your monetary wealth with those less fortunate. Of course, there are other ways to help those in need, like the sharing of your time or your skills. In Hebrew this is called Gemilut Ḥasadim (acts of kindness). The Talmud specifies many caring acts, such as

1. visiting the sick
2. comforting the mourner
3. housing the homeless

Right now you are a student, and even if you work outside of school, at this point your income is probably quite modest. Beyond the giving of money, think of some of the ways you can fulfill the responsibility of helping other people.

Working at a food donation center is one way to practice charity.

In Our Ancestors' Footsteps

Maimonides

Like Albert Einstein, Moses Maimonides became a famous man in his own day. Maimonides, an esteemed rabbi, philosopher, author, physician, and community leader, is considered by many to be one of the greatest figures in the history of the Jewish people. His two most important works, the *Mishneh Torah* (a code of all the laws of Judaism) and *The Guide to the Perplexed* (a book of philosophy), are still studied regularly throughout the Jewish world.

Maimonides (1135-1204) lived in Spain but was forced, like Einstein, to flee his native country. He sought refuge first in Morocco and then in Egypt. Maimonides wrote about how demanding his job was as physician to the royal family in Egypt. He described how he would stay up until all hours of the night helping people in need. As a rabbi and doctor, he helped many people in person and many others through letters he wrote to various Jewish communities throughout the world. In the same manner as Einstein, Maimonides found time, through sheer determination and tremendous stamina, to accomplish so much beyond his important everyday work.

In his writings, Maimonides discusses different levels ("a ladder") of observing the mitzvah of Tzedakah. In his opinion, the order of giving is this:

What are some examples of Maimonides' different levels of Tzedakah?

1. The person who gives reluctantly and with regret.
2. The person who gives graciously, but less than one should.
3. The person who gives what one should, but only after being asked.
4. The person who gives before being asked.
5. The person who gives without knowing to whom it is given, although the recipient knows the identity of the donor.
6. The person who gives without making his or her identity known.
7. The person who gives without knowing to whom it is given; the recipient does not know from whom he or she receives.
8. The person who helps another to become self-supporting through a gift or a loan or by finding employment for that person.

Spotlight on the Bible: Ruth

Perhaps the most beautiful story of Tzedakah in the Bible is found in the book of Ruth.

Ruth was not a Jew. She was a Moabite, but she married a Jew who had moved to Moab with his mother. Ruth's husband died, and soon after a famine struck the land of Moab. Ruth was devoted to her widowed mother-in-law, Naomi, and went with her to Bethlehem in the hope of finding some barley.

Ruth worked hard in the fields owned by a Jew named Boaz, gleaning what his reapers had left behind. When Boaz heard the story of Ruth's background, he ordered the young men who were doing the harvesting not to harm her, and he made sure she had water to drink. At mealtime he shared his food with her. Recognizing her goodness, he also gave her grain that his reapers had gathered.

Boaz acted out of charity, but his charity developed into love. Boaz and Ruth were married and had a son. That child became the grandfather of King David.

There are many other stories in the Bible of Tzedakah turning to love. *Can you think of one that involves Isaac and Rebecca?*

You Are There

America is in the midst of the Great Depression (the mid-1930s), and you are a prominent surgeon in New York. Not only is your caseload heavy, but you are attempting to publish some important papers in your field.

One day at a doctors' conference you are surprised to see Professor Albert Einstein approaching you. You are even more surprised when he asks you to join him to form an organization helping Jewish physicians leave Nazi Germany.

You are happy to give money, but you express your surprise that Einstein, who clearly has an extremely full schedule himself, is willing to devote his time and energy to this project.

Discuss how you think the conversation with Einstein might go.

～ *Jewish Heroes Hall of Fame* ～
Complete page 111 in the Jewish Heroes Hall of Fame.

---

11 SHALOM שָׁלוֹם

THE MITZVAH OF PEACE

"And they shall beat their swords into plowshares and their spears into pruning hooks. Nation shall not lift up sword against nation; neither shall they learn war anymore."

—ISAIAH 2:4

Israeli Prime Minister Yitzhak Rabin (left) shakes the hand of Jordan's King Hussein, signaling an end to nearly 50 years of war between Israel and Jordan.

Shalom is the mitzvah of making peace. The Hebrew word *shalom* comes from a root meaning "complete," or "whole." Confrontation fragments and divides people; peace restores and unifies.

THE PATH TO PEACE

Time: March 26, 1979
Place: The White House Lawn, Washington, D.C.
People: *Anwar el-Sadat*: the president of Egypt;
Menachem Begin: the prime minister of Israel;
Jimmy Carter: the president of the United States

Israel and Egypt fought four wars between 1948 and 1973. Then in November 1977, just a few months after Israel had elected a new government headed by Menachem Begin, Anwar el-Sadat electrified his Egyptian parliament when he announced in an address:

> I am ready to go to the end of the world to get a settlement. I am even ready to go to Israel, to the Knesset, and speak to all the members of the Israeli parliament there and negotiate with them over a peace settlement. . . . The Israelis are going to be stunned when they hear that I am ready to meet them in their home.

Negotiations at Camp David were not always placid, but Begin and Sadat got to know one another better—and to trust one another.

Seated at the table, signing the Israeli-Egyptian peace treaty, are Anwar el-Sadat, Jimmy Carter, and Menachem Begin.

The Israelis were stunned. They knew Sadat as the man whom the British had imprisoned during World War II for acts of terrorism, and they knew of his sympathy for the Nazis. In 1973, just four years before he made this address, Sadat had launched the bloodiest war in Israeli history. His troops attacked Israel on the holiest day of the year, Yom Kippur; the Egyptian forces inflicted severe damage on Israeli troops, equipment, and pride. Israel fought back valiantly and had regained the upper hand in the fighting when international powers imposed a truce.

Menachem Begin had also engaged in terrorist acts, in the years before the founding of Israel. For 30 years, he had been the leader of the opposition party, loudly decrying attempts by Knesset members to hold negotiations with the Arabs.

Still, the same day Sadat made his offer, Begin responded that Israel would welcome him with full honors. Begin offered a formal written invitation within 24 hours and made a radio and television broadcast to the Egyptian public urging "no more wars, no more bloodshed."

Two days later Anwar el-Sadat made a dramatic visit to Jerusalem. When he returned to Egypt, Sadat wrote in the diary, "I will stand by my peace initiative, whatever happens."

Difficult Negotiations

Despite Sadat's visit, and subsequent meetings between the leaders of Israel and Egypt, peace negotiations began to fall apart. President Jimmy Carter then decided that the only way to revive the peace talks was to personally invite Begin and Sadat to his presidential retreat in the mountains of Maryland, called Camp David.

What risks were Begin and Sadat willing to take to achieve peace?

Carter, a former governor of Georgia, was not considered to have particular expertise in foreign affairs. Nevertheless, he kept Sadat, Begin, and their bargaining teams at the table for 13 days and nights. Their perseverance was rewarded, and an agreement was announced on September 17, 1978. Soon afterward, Begin and Sadat were awarded the Nobel Peace Prize for their breakthrough.

The three leaders converged at the White House on March 26, 1979, to sign the peace treaty, which became known as the Camp David Accords. Excerpts from the speeches of the three leaders at this momentous occasion follow in the next section.

In October of 1981, Sadat was assassinated by opponents of the peace treaty. But the peace held, and it continues to do so to this day.

Eyewitness to History

Below are excerpts from addresses delivered at the White House Lawn on March 26, 1979.

President Carter:

Today we celebrate a victory, not of a bloody military campaign, but of an inspiring peace campaign. Two leaders who loom large in the history of nations, President Anwar Sadat and Prime Minister Menachem Begin, have conducted this campaign with all the courage, tenacity, brilliance, and inspiration of any generals who have ever led men and machines onto the field of battle. . . .

Let those who would shatter peace, who would callously spill more blood, be aware that we three and all others who may join us will vigorously wage peace. So let history record that deep and ancient antagonisms can be settled without bloodshed.

President Sadat:

Let there be no more war or bloodshed between Arabs and the Israelis. Let there be no more suffering or denial of rights. Let there be no more despair or loss of faith. Let no mother lament the loss of her child. Let no young man waste his life on a conflict from which no one benefits. Let us work together until the day comes when they beat their swords into plowshares and their spears into pruning hooks; and God does call to the abode of peace.

Prime Minister Begin:

The ancient Jewish people gave the world the vision of eternal peace, of universal disarmament, of abolishing the teaching and learning of war. . . . Despite the tragedies and disappointments of the past, we must never forsake that vision, that human dream, that unshakable faith. Peace is the beauty of life. It is sunshine. It is the smile of a child, the love of a mother, the joy of a father, the togetherness of a family. It is the advancement of man, the victory of a just cause, the triumph of truth. Peace is all of these and more, and more.

Now is the time for all of us to show civil courage in order to proclaim to our peoples, and to others: no more war, no more bloodshed, no more bereavement—peace unto you. Shalom, Salaam—forever.

Exploring the Mitzvah

Shalom

"The work of the righteous is peace." —Isaiah 32:17

What qualities define a peacemaker?

Shalom is one of the most important words in the Jewish vocabulary. We greet a person with the word *shalom*. We say good-bye with the same word. On the Sabbath, we say *Shabbat Shalom*. We conclude many of our most important prayers, such as the Kaddish, Birkat Hamazon (grace after meals), and the Priestly Blessing, with a plea for peace. We also conclude the Amidah, the prayers that make up the heart of the daily and Sabbath service, with a prayer for peace. According to the Talmud, Shalom is one of the names of God. Rabbi Shim'on ben Gamliel is often quoted: "By three things the world is preserved: by truth, by judgment, and by peace" (Avot 1:18).

Our tradition teaches that the mitzvah of Shalom can be fulfilled on a number of different levels. Peacemaking begins in our very own family. Judaism has a special expression for the kind of peace that describes family harmony. It is called *sh'lom bayit*, which means "peace of the home."

Think about your own family. Now name some things you can do to increase *sh'lom bayit*.

Pursuing peace also takes place in your community, be it among friends, at school, or in the workplace. Here again the sages coined an expression, *mipnei darchei shalom*, meaning "for the sake of peace." The rabbis urged that sometimes we should do things, even if we are not required to, or even if we do not feel like it, just for the sake of peace.

In thinking about your relationships with friends or associates, is there something you can do for someone that is "beyond the call of duty" but that will add Shalom to your community?

LIVING THE MITZVAH

Help create sh'lom bayit (peace in the home).

Talk to your parents about what steps might enhance *sh'lom bayit* in your own family. Is there anyone you need to apologize to—a brother, a sister, a parent? What about offering to make dinner one night a week?

Finally, there is the kind of Shalom brought about by Menachem Begin and Anwar el-Sadat. This is the peace between nations. As Israeli Prime Minister Yitzhak Rabin said when he signed his treaty with Yasir Arafat, chairman of the Palestine Liberation Organization, "Peace is something you make with your enemies."

Enemies do not become friends overnight, however. In the beginning, peace between nations is often simply the avoidance of war. The term "cold peace" was used to describe the relations between Egypt and Israel after the treaty signing. Israel publicly expressed the wish that the relations between the two countries would evolve into a "warm peace" that included things like mutual trade, tourism, and cultural exchanges. Such peace can often take generations, and it has not yet fully blossomed. As Albert Einstein once wrote, "Peace cannot be kept by force. It can only be achieved by understanding."

A modern Jewish prayerbook contains an especially beautiful plea for peace: "Grant us peace, O eternal Source of peace, and enable Israel to be its messenger unto the peoples of the earth. Bless our country that it may ever be a stronghold of peace and its advocate in the council of nations."

In Our Ancestors' Footsteps

Jews and the Nobel Peace Prize

When Menachem Begin shared the Nobel Peace Prize with Anwar el-Sadat in 1978, he became the fourth Jew to receive this great international award, which is given to men and women who have "rendered the greatest service to mankind."

Elie Wiesel won the Nobel Peace Prize in 1986.

In 1911 two Jews shared the award: Alfred Fried, an Austrian author and a leader of the international peace movement, and Tobias Asser, a Dutch jurist who specialized in international law and arbitration.

In 1968 the Peace Prize was awarded to French jurist René Cassin, one of the principle drafters of the Universal Declaration of Human Rights.

Elie Wiesel was awarded the Nobel Peace Prize in 1986. The author of more than 30 books, Wiesel has dedicated his life to bearing witness to the Holocaust, which he survived, and to preventing genocide from taking place again.

In 1994 the Nobel Peace Prize was awarded to Yitzhak Rabin, the prime minister of Israel, Shimon Peres, Israel's foreign minister, and Yasir Arafat, the chairman of the Palestine Liberation Organization. Israel's ability to sign a peace treaty with the PLO was a direct consequence of the treaty signed by Begin and Sadat. Israel has also signed a peace treaty with Jordan as a result, and established peaceful relationships with other Arab and non-Arab Muslim countries as well.

SPOTLIGHT ON THE BIBLE: AARON

In Jewish tradition, Aaron (brother of Moses and the first high priest) is portrayed as the ideal "man of peace." This portrayal is based not so much on Aaron's actions in the Torah, but on the legends about him recorded in the Midrash. In Pirkei Avot, which is part of the Talmud, we read a famous line: "Be of the disciples of Aaron, loving peace and pursuing it."

An early commentary to Pirkei Avot (Avot D'Rabbi Natan, Chap. 12) teaches that Aaron had two outstanding characteristics. Aaron would always greet people he met, even if he knew they were evil, in the hopes of helping them become better people. Aaron would likewise intervene when he saw people quarreling, and convince them to listen to each other. The sages explain that Aaron would sit with each side separately and enable them to recognize that their adversary sought reconciliation. "And when the two met each other, they would embrace and kiss each other."

According to the Midrash, "That is why (of Aaron's death) it is said, 'They wept for Aaron thirty days, even all the house of Israel.'" The sages go on to say that Aaron's commitment to peace made him beloved. Moses, to their mind, was deserving of the deepest respect. But Aaron won a special place of love in the people's hearts because he was a peacemaker.

You Are There

Imagine you are President Carter, sitting down with Anwar el-Sadat and Menachem Begin at Camp David. You have been negotiating for days, but now you're at an impasse. Both men have said they can do no more; they're ready to give up and go home.

What do you say to keep them at the table? Do you threaten them financially? What rewards can you suggest to keep them negotiating? Are there any options that you keep up your sleeve for later? How do you make others want peace as much as you do?

LIVING THE MITZVAH

Honor a peacemaker.

Learn about a leader who is trying to bring peace to a troubled part of the world. Make a small report to the class about the efforts of that person. You could even write a letter of support to that leader.

⬿ Jewish Heroes Hall of Fame ⬿

Complete page 112 in the Jewish Heroes Hall of Fame.

---

12 ZIKARON זִכָּרוֹן

THE MITZVAH OF REMEMBRANCE

"We believe that memory is the answer—perhaps the only answer."
—ELIE WIESEL

Steven Spielberg directing Liam Neeson, who played Oskar Schindler in the film *Schindler's List*.

Zikaron is the mitzvah of remembrance. For the Jews, remembering the past has always been a sacred responsibility. Memory links us to generations past and helps inspire us to face the future.

THE MAKING OF SCHINDLER'S LIST

Setting the Scene ✳ ✳ ✳ ✳ ✳

Time: December 1993

Place: Movie theaters throughout the county

People: *Steven Spielberg*: one of the most successful movie directors of all time;

Oskar Schindler: an Austrian businessman;

Leopold Pfefferberg: a Jewish Holocaust survivor;

Thomas Keneally: an Australian novelist

In 1947, a Polish Jew named Leopold Pfefferberg, who had survived the Holocaust, made a vow to make the story of Oskar Schindler famous. Schindler was a complex and contradictory man—an Austrian businessman and Nazi party member with a reputation for drinking and gambling. Yet Schindler, through every means possible and at risk to his own life, managed to convince the Nazi authorities not to harm the Jews who worked at his factory. As a result, more than 1,000 Jews escaped certain death in the concentration camps.

In this scene from *Schindler's List*, Liam Neeson looks over the shoulder of Ben Kingsley, who is typing a list of more than 1,000 Jewish workers to be placed under Schindler's protection.

The real Oskar Schindler.

Leopold Pfefferberg eventually settled in Los Angeles, where he opened a luggage and handbag shop. One day in 1980 an Australian writer, Thomas Keneally, happened to stop in. Pfefferberg asked him what he was doing in this part of the world. Keneally replied that he was a writer on a book-signing tour. When Pfefferberg heard that, he said, "You are a writer? I have a story for you."

Keneally was intrigued. He spent several years doing research. When *Schindler's List* was published, people were astonished by the story. The book was a best-seller and Keneally won several awards. In 1982, a proposal for a screenplay was brought to Steven Spielberg.

The Right Man for the Job

Why did Steven Spielberg hesitate to make Schindler's List? What changed his mind?

Spielberg had directed four of the ten top-grossing movies of all time: *Jurassic Park* (#1), *E.T.* (#2), *Indiana Jones: The Last Crusade* (#5), and *Jaws* (#8). Though born and raised as a Jew, Spielberg had little connection with, and conflicting feelings about, his Jewish roots. Nevertheless, he made a tentative commitment to the project. Other film projects intervened, however, and Spielberg did not like the scripts he saw. Finally, nearly a decade (and three screenwriters) later, Spielberg was ready to make the movie.

It proved to be an unforgettable experience for him, for all those involved in the film, and for millions of viewers. In the next section Steven Spielberg relates how he came to his personal act of remembrance.

Eyewitness to History

This account of Steven Spielberg's childhood and his decision to make *Schindler's List* is drawn from interviews in *Time, Newsweek, The New York Times, The Jerusalem Report, Hadassah Magazine,* and *Premiere*.

[The film] is a remembrance for the survivors, for my mother's generation, and the people who should learn more. . . . With the ugliness reemerging in Eastern Europe and all over Europe . . . I think it's a good time for this movie to be seen. These events occurred only 50 years ago. And it could happen in all its monstrosity again.

I am doing service, for the first time, to my Jewishness. . . . [Growing up] I kept wanting to have Christmas lights on the front of our house so it didn't look like the Black Hole of Calcutta in an all-Gentile neighbor-

Steven Spielberg holding two Oscars that he won for *Schindler's List* for best director and best picture.

What effect did the making of Schindler's List have on Spielberg?

hood. I would beg my father, "Dad, please let us have some lights," and he'd say, "No, we're Jewish," and I'd say, "What about taking that white porch light out and screwing in a red porch light?" and he'd say, "No!" and I'd say, "What about a yellow porch light?" and he said, "No!"

When we moved to Phoenix, I was one of only five Jewish kids in elementary and high school. There was a lot of anti-Semitism against me and my sisters. In study hall kids used to pitch pennies at me, which would hit my desk and make a large clatter. It was called "pitching pennies at the Jew" and it was very hurtful. People coughed the word "Jew" in their hand as they passed me in the hallway. I got smacked and kicked to the ground during physical education, in the locker room. . . . I was an outsider, and as a result I wasn't proud of my Jewish heritage—I was ashamed.

I was so ashamed of being a Jew, and now I'm filled with pride. I don't even know when that transition happened.

I felt so helpless [after my first visit to Auschwitz] that there was nothing I could do about it. And yet, I thought, well there is something I can do about it. I can make *Schindler's List*. I mean, I'm not going to bring anybody back alive, but it maybe will remind others that another Holocaust is a sad possibility.

I was frightened every day [of the filming]. . . . I go to Poland and I get hit in the face with my personal life. My upbringing. My Jewishness. The stories my grandparents told me about the Shoah. And Jewish life came pouring back into my heart. I cried all the time. I never cry on sets making films. . . . I recreated these events, and then I experienced them as any witness or victim would have. It wasn't like a movie.

Exploring the Mitzvah

Zikaron

"Remember the days of old." —DEUTERONOMY 32:7

LIVING THE MITZVAH

Help your family "to remember."

Create a family history album. Add a special element by interviewing your parents and grand-parents and other relatives about their Jewish memories, and include some of their best stories in your project.

Ever since we became a people, we have been commanded to remember our history. In fact, the Torah uses the term "remember" over 200 times! The Israelites are told to remember everything important— both the good (such as the Exodus from Egypt) and the bad (such as the Amalekites, Israel's worst enemy in the time of Joshua). Repeatedly, the people are urged to remember the ways in which God has sustained them and the responsibilities God has placed before them.

Perhaps the most significant way that Judaism fulfills the responsibility to remember its history is by making the reading of the Torah the center-piece of every Shabbat-morning worship. In the middle of our prayer, we pause for a history lesson. Week after week, year after year, we retell the ancient stories of our people. The same principle applies at the Pesaḥ seder, when in response to the Four Questions, we interrupt our prayers to retell the story of our liberation.

The importance of memory is emphasized numerous times during the Passover seder.

Why is remembering history so important? The philosopher George Santayana gave a now classic reply: "Those who cannot learn from the past are condemned to repeat it." Judaism agrees that wisdom can spring from memory.

Elie Wiesel, a survivor of the Holocaust and a man who has dedicated his life to remembering and bearing witness, remarked to President Ronald Reagan:

> When I write, I feel my invisible teachers standing over my shoulders, reading my words, and judging their veracity. And while I feel responsible for the living, I feel equally responsible to the dead. Their memory dwells in my memory.

There is another important way that Judaism fulfills the mitzvah of Zikaron. Before the end of every service we pause to say a prayer called the Kaddish. Kaddish is recited in memory of our loved ones. It is customary before the Kaddish to read aloud the names of those in the congregation who have recently passed on, or those for whom this date is the anniversary of their death (called the *yahrzeit*). By reading aloud these names year after year, we help ensure that those individuals will never be forgotten. As an author once wrote, "How can a people that remembers its past generations ever disappear?"

Ask your parents or grandparents for whom they say Kaddish.

In many Jewish families it is also customary to help keep alive the memory of a loved one by naming a child after that person. *Find out if you are named after a relative. What about your brothers, sisters, and parents?*

Another example of the importance of remembrance in Judaism is Shabbat. The special day itself is considered to be a double reminder. When we raise the wine cup for the Shabbat evening Kiddush, we call Shabbat a *zikaron l'maaseh v'reishit* ("remembrance of creation"), and at the same time a *zecher liy'tziyat mitzrayim* ("reminder of the Exodus"). Observing Shabbat encourages us to remember our role in the great design of God's universe, and to remember that the freedom we enjoy is a great gift that we once were denied.

The Jewish responsibility of remembrance is fulfilled in many ways: by retelling our history (in such varied ways as chanting the Torah, writing a book, or making a movie), by observing Shabbat and the holidays, by saying Kaddish, or by naming our children. Through remembering we help ensure that Judaism will be passed *dor l'dor*, from generation to generation. Through remembrance we ensure that we, and the world, will learn from history.

LIVING THE MITZVAH

Learn about our people's history.

Read a book about Jewish history. Would you prefer a biography or a historical novel? Would you like to read about someone mentioned in this book? Ask your librarian, teacher, or rabbi for a few suggestions.

In Our Ancestors' Footsteps

The Righteous of the Nations

In Israel and the Jewish world, Oskar Schindler is known as one of the "righteous of the nations" (in Hebrew, *ḥasidei ummot ha-olam*). It is a term applied to those non-Jews who risked their lives to save Jews from the Nazis during the Holocaust. For Jews, part of the mitzvah of Zikaron is preserving the memory of these heroic people.

In 1953, the Israeli Knesset officially passed legislation creating Yad Vashem, Israel's Holocaust Remembrance Center. One of its charges is to perpetuate the names of "the high-minded righteous who risked their lives to save Jews." A commission was appointed to check every instance of a Holocaust rescuer whose name was submitted for official recognition. A special walkway at Yad Vashem was created, called the Avenue of the Righteous, and there a tree is planted in memory of the rescuer. Those qualifying for the highest honor also receive a medal and certificate.

Hundreds of trees have been planted along the Avenue of the Righteous at Yad Vashem on Har HaZikaron (the Hill of Remembrance). There are trees honoring individuals, like Oskar Schindler, and Raoul Wallenberg, a Swedish diplomat who is credited with saving many thousands of Jews. There are also trees honoring whole groups of people, like the Danish underground. During World War II almost all of Denmark's Jews were safely evacuated because of the bravery of the Danish people. Altogether, over 8,000 men and women have been identified by Yad Vashem as right-

In what ways can the Jews be described as "a people that never forgets"?

Yad Vashem, established in Jerusalem in 1953, stands as a memorial museum and library for the 6 million Jews lost in the Holocaust.

eous of the nations, and their rescue efforts verified. Discovering and honoring the righteous of the nations is a process that continues even today.

SPOTLIGHT ON THE BIBLE: EXODUS

One line in the Bible sums up the importance of memory:

"And there arose a new king who knew not Joseph." (Exodus 1:8).

If Pharaoh had only been reminded of how Joseph had been of service to the old ruler, perhaps the entire story of the Exodus might never have happened. But Pharaoh was not reminded, and the Israelites were treated as if they were a threat to the Egyptians. How much harsher the Israelites must have considered their treatment by Pharaoh when they remembered that they had originally been invited into the country and that they had been of benefit to the Egyptian rulers in the past!

Medieval rabbis asked, "Why did Pharaoh need ten plagues before he made up his mind to let the Jews go?" In a midrash, they suggested that Pharaoh forgot how calamitous each plague was after it was over. Unable to recall the pain once it was no longer felt, he hardened his heart and refused Moses' command to "Let My people go!"

As we retell the lessons of the Exodus each year, so should we remind ourselves of the danger of forgetting.

You Are There

Imagine you were Leopold Pfefferberg. You and some friends have survived the Holocaust, even though most of your other friends and family have perished in the concentration camps. The story of your survival—and the survival of over 1,000 other Jews—is amazing, yet virtually no one else knows that story.

For 35 years you lived with this piece of history welling up inside you. How would you feel? Would you want to tell everyone, or would you be afraid of being thought of as a crank or a bore? Whom would you want to know your story?

Do you think your parents and grandparents also have stories that they need others to know?

~ Jewish Heroes Hall of Fame ~
Complete page 113 in the Jewish Heroes Hall of Fame.

Jewish Heroes Hall of Fame

The people pictured on the following pages embody the ideals and values of our tradition.

Beneath each picture, the contribution of the hero is left blank. You can complete the Hall of Fame by writing the mitzvah each person fulfilled and how he or she fulfilled it.

At the bottom of each page, you can describe a way you can fulfill each mitzvah. For as you read at the beginning of this book, "Heroes start out as ordinary women and men. What makes them special is their determination to accept responsibility and live according to high ideals." You are now ready to begin your own journey to help repair and improve God's world.

RABBI YOḤANAN BEN ZAKKAI

> Give me Yavneh and its sages . . .
> so that we have a place to keep
> our heritage alive.
>
> **—Rabbi Yoḥanan ben Zakkai**

Rabbi Yoḥanan ben Zakkai fulfilled the mitzvah of _____ by _____
_____
_____

I can fulfill this mitzvah by _____
_____
_____
_____

Hall of Fame

SANDY KOUFAX

> There was never any decision to make because there was never any possibility that I would pitch. Yom Kippur is the holiest day of the Jewish religion. The club knows that I don't work that day.
>
> —Sandy Koufax

Sandy Koufax fulfilled the mitzvah of _____ by _____

_____

_____

_____

I can fulfill this mitzvah by _____

_____

_____

_____

GOLDA MEIR

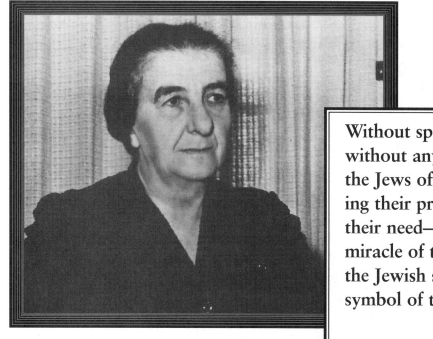

> Without speeches or parades, without any words at all really, the Jews of Moscow were proving their profound desire—and their need—to participate in the miracle of the establishment of the Jewish state, and I was the symbol of the state for them.
>
> **—Golda Meir**

Golda Meir fulfilled the mitzvah of_____ by _____

_____

_____

I can fulfill this mitzvah by _____

_____

_____

_____

RABBI ABRAHAM JOSHUA HESCHEL

> As surely as we are driven to live, we are driven to serve spiritual ends that surpass our own interests.
>
> —**Rabbi Abraham Joshua Heschel**

Rabbi Abraham Joshua Heschel fulfilled the mitzvah of_____ by_____

_____

_____

_____

I can fulfill this mitzvah by _____

_____

_____

_____

ROSE SCHNEIDERMAN

> I know from my experience, it is up to the working people to save themselves.
>
> **—Rose Schneiderman**

Rose Schneiderman fulfilled the mitzvah of_____ by_____

_____

_____

I can fulfill this mitzvah by _____

_____

_____

_____

Hall of Fame

HANNAH SENESH

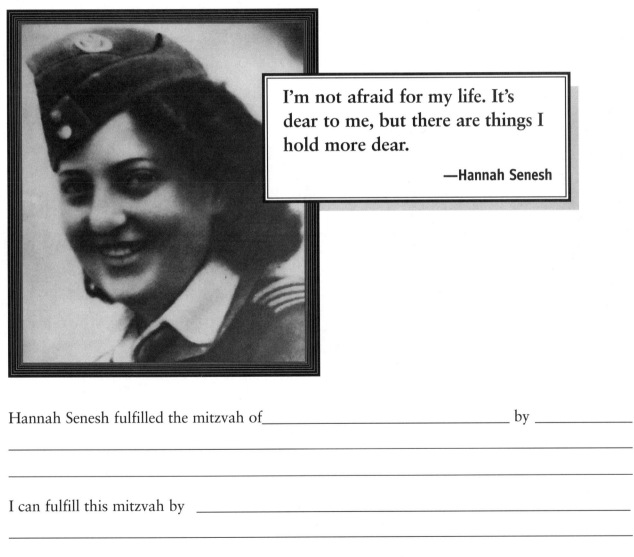

> I'm not afraid for my life. It's dear to me, but there are things I hold more dear.
>
> **—Hannah Senesh**

Hannah Senesh fulfilled the mitzvah of_____ by _____

_____

_____

I can fulfill this mitzvah by _____

_____

_____

_____

Jewish Heroes

AVITAL AND NATAN SHARANSKY

> I am happy that I helped people. I am proud that I knew and worked with such honest, brave, and courageous people. I am fortunate to have been witness to the process of the liberation of Jews of the USSR.
>
> **—Natan Sharansky**

Avital and Natan Sharansky fulfilled the mitzvah of _____ by _____

_____

_____

_____

I can fulfill this mitzvah by _____

_____

_____

_____

ANNE FRANK

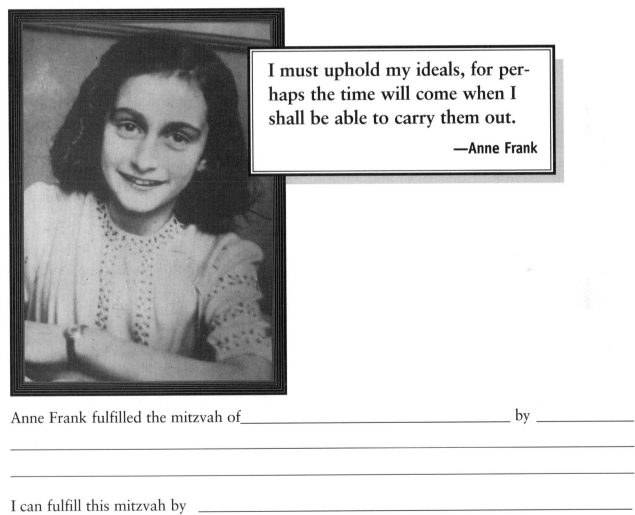

> I must uphold my ideals, for perhaps the time will come when I shall be able to carry them out.
>
> —Anne Frank

Anne Frank fulfilled the mitzvah of _____ by _____

_____

_____

I can fulfill this mitzvah by _____

_____

_____

_____

RUTH BADER GINSBURG

> I would like the legislature of this country to stand up and say, "We want to make a clarion call that women and men are equal before the law."
>
> —Ruth Bader Ginsburg

Ruth Bader Ginsburg fulfilled the mitzvah of_____ by _____

_____

_____

_____

I can fulfill this mitzvah by _____

_____

_____

_____

Hall of Fame

YONATAN NETANYAHU

> I am doing things because they have to be done. . . . I have an obligation not only to the job but to myself as well.
>
> **—Yonatan Netanyahu**

Yonatan Netanyahu fulfilled the mitzvah of_____ by _____

_____

_____

_____

I can fulfill this mitzvah by _____

_____

_____

_____

HENRIETTA SZOLD

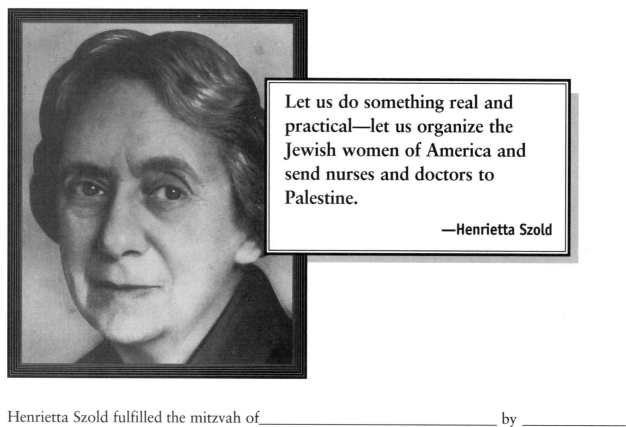

> Let us do something real and practical—let us organize the Jewish women of America and send nurses and doctors to Palestine.
>
> **—Henrietta Szold**

Henrietta Szold fulfilled the mitzvah of _____ by _____

_____

_____

I can fulfill this mitzvah by _____

_____

_____

_____

ALBERT EINSTEIN

> The life of the individual has meaning only insofar as it aids in making the life of every living thing nobler and more beautiful.
>
> **—Albert Einstein**

Albert Einstein fulfilled the mitzvah of_____ by_____

_____

_____

_____

I can fulfill this mitzvah by _____

_____

_____

_____

MENACHEM BEGIN

> Now is the time for all of us to show civil courage in order to proclaim to our peoples, and to others: no more war, no more bloodshed, no more bereavement—peace unto you.
>
> —Menachem Begin

Menachem Begin fulfilled the mitzvah of_____ by_____

_____

_____

I can fulfill this mitzvah by _____

_____

_____

_____

Hall of Fame

STEVEN SPIELBERG

> The film is a remembrance for the survivors, for my mother's generation, and the people who should learn more. I am doing service, for the first time, to my Jewishness.
>
> —**Steven Spielberg**

Steven Spielberg fulfilled the mitzvah of_____ by _____

_____

_____

_____

I can fulfill this mitzvah by _____

_____

_____

_____

SOURCES

Extracts that appear in the Eyewitness to History sections and elsewhere in this book may be found in the following sources.

Chapter 1
Babylonian Talmud, Gittin 56.

Chapter 2
Sandy Koufax with Ed Linn. *Koufax*. New York: Viking Press, 1966, pp. 258-259.

Chapter 3
Golda Meir. *My Life*. New York: Dell Publishing Co., 1975, pp. 240-241.

Chapter 4
Ruth Marcus Goodhill, ed. *The Wisdom of Heschel*. New York: Farrar, Straus & Giroux, 1975.

John C. Merkle, ed. *Abraham Joshua Heschel: Exploring His Life and Thought*. New York: Macmillan, 1985, pp. 9, 129, 130-131, 133.

Chapter 5
Hannah Senesh. *Her Life and Diary*. New York: Schocken, 1971, pp. 172-174, 176-177, 190, 193.

Chapter 6
Francine Klagsbrun. *Voices of Wisdom*. New York: Pantheon Books, 1980, p. 374.

Natan Sharansky. *Fear No Evil*. New York: Random House, 1988, p. 244.

Chapter 7
Anne Frank. *The Diary of Anne Frank*. Critical Edition. New York: Doubleday, 1989.

Elie Wiesel. *A Jew Today*. New York: Random House, 1978, pp. 145-149.

Chapter 8
New York Times, June 15-16, 1993; July 21-23, 1993.

Chapter 9
Max Hastings. *Yoni, Hero of Entebbe*. New York: Dial Press, 1979.

Chapter 10

Albert Einstein. *The World As I See It*. New York: Philosophical Library, 1949, pp. 90, 91, 93, 106.

Albert Einstein. *Einstein on Peace*. New York: Schocken, 1960, p. 263.

Chapter 11

The Camp David Accords. Washington, D.C.: Embassy of Israel, 1979.

Chapter 12

New York Times, December 12, 1993; *Hadassah Magazine*, December 1993; *Premiere*, January 1994; *Newsweek*, December 20, 1993; *Jerusalem Report*, December 30, 1993.

Elie Wiesel quoted in Geoffrey H. Hartman, ed. *Bitburg in Moral and Political Perspective*. Bloomington: Indiana University Press, 1986, p. 241.

KEEP READING

A selected bibliography about some of the people and events mentioned in this book.

Chapter 2—Sandy Koufax
Grabowski, John. *Sandy Koufax*. New York: Chelsea House, 1992. (Leader series)

Halo, Arnold. *Sandy Koufax: Strikeout King*. New York: G.P. Putnam's Sons, 1964.

Slater, Robert. *Great Jews in Sports*. New York: Jonathan David, 1983.

Chapter 3—Golda Meir
Adler, David. *Our Golda: The Story of Golda Meir*. New York: Puffin Books, 1984.

Amdur, Richard. *Golda Meir, A Leader in Peace and War*. New York: Fawcett, 1990.

Dobrin, Arnold. *A Life for Israel: The Story of Golda Meir*. New York: Dial Books, 1974.

McAuley, Karen. *Golda Meir*. New York, Chelsea House, 1985. (Leader series)

Chapter 5—Hannah Senesh
Atkinson, Linda. *In Kindling Flame: The Story of Hannah Senesh*. New York: Lothrop, Lee and Shepard, 1983.

Chapter 6—Natan and Avital Sharansky
Anatoly and Avital Sharansky: The Journey Home. (Jerusalem Post, ed.) San Diego: Harcourt Brace, 1986.

Gilbert, Martin. *Sharansky: Hero of our Time*. New York: Viking, 1986.

Sharansky, Natan. *Fear No Evil*. New York: Random House, 1989.

Chapter 7—Anne Frank and the Holocaust
Amdur, Richard. *Anne Frank*. New York: Chelsea House, 1992. (Leader series)

Frank, Anne. *The Diary of a Young Girl*. New York, Random House, 1952.

Hurwitz, Johanna. *Anne Frank; Life in Hiding*. Philadelphia: Jewish Publication Society, 1988.

Chapter 9—Yonatan Netanyahu and Entebbe
Peck, Ira. *Raid at Entebbe*. New York: Scholastic Books, 1977.

Stevenson, William. *90 Minutes at Entebbe*. New York: Bantam, 1976.

Chapter 10—Albert Einstein

Dank, Milton. *Albert Einstein*. PLB, 1983. (Impact biography series)

Wise, William. *Albert Einstein: Citizen of the World*. Philadelphia, Jewish Publication Society, 1960.

Chapter 11—Menachem Begin

Amdur, Richard. *Menachem Begin*. New York: Chelsea House, 1988. (Leader series)

Pitch, Anthony. *Peace*. West Englewood, N.J.: SBS Publishing, 1979.

Chapter 12—Oskar Schindler

Keneally, Thomas. *Schindler's List*. New York: Simon and Schuster, 1992.

INDEX